Glamorgan Lost Railways

Peter Dale

Clydach-on-Tawe Station, *c.* 1910.

Stenlake Publishing Ltd

© 2014 Peter Dale
First Published in the United Kingdom, 2014
Stenlake Publishing Limited
54-58 Mill Square, Catrine, KA5 6RD
01290 551122
www.stenlake.co.uk

ISBN 9781840336740

A train heads towards Mumbles on the Swansea & Mumbles Railway, May 1959.

Acknowledgements

The publishers wish to thank the following for contributing photographs to this book: John Alsop for the front and back covers, also the inside front cover (lower) and inside back cover (both) as well as pages 1, 3, 5 (both), 7 (upper), 11 (upper), 12, 13 (both), 14 (lower), 17 (lower), 22, 24 (both), 25 (lower), 27 (upper), 28, 31 (lower), 32 (lower), 33 (upper), 34, 36, 37 (upper), 38 (lower), 39 (upper), 44, 46 (upper), 48, 49, 50 (upper), 51 (both), 52 (both), 53, 54, 56, 58 (both), 60 (upper), 62 (both), 63 (both), 64 (lower), 65, 68 (both), 69 (upper), 71, 73 (lower), 75 (lower), 78 (upper), 79 (upper), 80 (both), 81 (both), 83 (centre), 84 (both), 85, 86, 88 (both), 90 (bottom), 94 (top), 96 (both), 97, 98, 99 (both), 100, 102, 105 (top), 106 (lower), 107, 108 (all), 109 (both), 110 (top), 111 (both) and 112 (both) ; and to Richard Casserley for the inside front cover (upper) and pages 6 (both), 7 (lower), 9 (both), 10 (both), 14 (upper), 15, 16 (both), 17 (upper), 18, 19, 20 (both), 21, 23, 25 (upper), 26 (both), 27 (lower), 30, 31 (upper), 32 (upper), 33 (lower), 37 (lower), 38 (upper), 39 (lower),41 (both), 43 (all), 46 (lower), 47 (both), 50 (lower), 57 (both), 59, 60 (lower), 61, 64 (upper), 67 (both), 69 (lower), 70 (both), 72, 73 (upper), 74, 75 (upper), 76 (both), 78 (lower), 79 (lower), 83 (top & bottom), 87 (both), 89, 90 (top & centre), 95 (centre), 101, 103 (both), 104, 105 (centre & bottom), 106 (upper) and 110 (bottom).

Introduction

Glamorgan is now part of the county of Gwent. Some of the earliest industrialisation of the area was to do with the smelting of tin and copper and consequently there were a considerable number of early tramroads or plateways in the area. In 1804 the great Cornish engineer, Trevithick, ran an early locomotive on one of these, while the area's other claim to fame in railway history is the Oystermouth Railway which ran the first passenger service in the world on 25 March 1807.

The broad gauge South Wales Railway ran roughly along the coast from Grange Court to Haverfordwest. After it was absorbed by the Great Western Railway in August 1863 that company dominated the area in railway terms. However, there were two other major railway companies in the area: the London & North Western Railway and the Midland Railway, the second and fourth largest companies respectively in terms of route mileage. Both of these companies gained access to South Wales from the north and this gave rise to some interesting route possibilities later on. Although the accepted route to South Wales from London is from Paddington, it used to be possible to also travel from Euston. Paddington to Swansea is 199 miles but Euston to Swansea via Stafford and Shrewsbury was 278 miles, but as some tickets were available for any route the fare was the same. The journey from Euston could be done without changing trains as a through coach was attached to The Manxman (Mondays to Fridays) and to The Welshman on a Saturday. It took seven hours and 55 minutes. For many years both the Midland and the Great Western provided a service, by separate routes, from Hereford to Swansea.

A term frequently used through this book is the 'Grouping' and an explanation of its significance is offered for non-railway enthusiasts here. Many of the railways in Britain were built by small companies, sometimes with the backing of a larger company. In the years leading up to 1923 there was a process of consolidation by which smaller companies amalgamated or were absorbed by larger ones, but in 1922 there were still well over 100 different railway companies in Britain. In 1923 all but a few minor companies were grouped into four larger concerns by Act of Parliament. They were the Great Western Railway (which continued in an enlarged form), the Southern Railway, the London Midland & Scottish Railway (which included the London & North Western and Midland railways) and the London & North Eastern Railway. These four companies – often referred to as the 'Big Four' – continued until nationalisation in 1948. Under British Railways a Modernisation Plan introduced in 1955 spelt the beginning of the end for steam on British Railways, while the Beeching Plan of 1963 saw the start of widespread closures of many minor, and some major, lines.

The area was unusual in that it had many smaller, but locally important, railways that kept their independence right up to the Grouping. In the years before this there was a lot of variety in both locomotives and liveries: around 1914 some of the liveries to be seen included those of the Taff Vale Railway (black locos with coaches painted chocolate with white upper panels), the Rhymney Railway (dark green locos and maroon coaches), the Great Western (green locos and crimson lake coaches), the Barry Railway (dark red locos and red coaches), the London & North Western Railway (black locos and purple/brown with white upper panels on coaches) and the Midland (crimson lake on both locos and coaches).

Although this book is concerned with passenger railways it should not be forgotten that there was also (and still is to a lesser extent) a large mileage of freight-only lines not only owned by the railway companies but also by collieries. Some years after main-line steam had finished small tank engines could still be seen doing a real job of work on lines then owned by the National Coal Board.

I hope this book will convey some of the fascination of an area provided with such a high density of railway mileage and diversity of companies at a time when the only alternative to the train (and then only over short distances) was the electric street tramway of which there were several in the area.

A Taff Vale rail motor stops at Cowbridge Station, *c.* 1908. To the left of the station and above the sign advertising Lipton's Tea is the low shed of the old station which closed in 1892 when the line was extended to Aberthaw.

Alexandra (Newport & South Wales) Docks & Railway

Passenger service withdrawn	17 September 1956
Distance	5.2 miles
Company	Pontypridd, Caerphilly & Newport Railway

Stations closed	*Date of closure*
Pontypridd Tram Road	10 July 1922
Glyntaff Halt *	5 May 1930
Treforest Halt **	17 September 1956
Rhyd-y-felin High Level Halt ***	2 February 1953
Dynea Halt ****	17 September 1956
Upper Boat Halt †	17 September 1956
Nantgarw Halt High Level ††	17 September 1956

*	Known as Glyntaff until 1 July 1924.
**	Known as Treforest until 1 July 1924.
***	This station replaced an earlier station of the same name about 400 yards to the west on 1 July 1924. That had been known as Rhyd-y-felin until 1 July 1924.
****	This halt (sometimes known as Dynes Halt) was known as Dynea until 1 July 1924.
†	Known as Upper Boat until 1 July 1924.
††	Known as Nantgarw until 1 July 1924.

The Alexandra (Newport) Dock Company was formed in 1865 but progress was slow and the North Dock and its connecting railway did not open until April 1875. The name of the company was changed to the Alexandra (Newport & South Wales) Dock & Railway in 1882.

The Pontypridd, Caerphilly & Newport Railway was formed to build a railway to carry coal from the Rhondda and Aberdare valleys to Newport for export. The line was built in two sections, from Pontypridd to Caerphilly and from Bassaleg to Mendalgyf Junction with the Alexandra Dock Railway. Running powers over the Brecon & Merthyr and Rhymney lines enabled trains to run between the two sections. Although it finally opened throughout in April 1886, no passenger service was provided on the line until 28 December 1887. The company owned neither locomotives or coaches so these were provided by the Alexandra Dock & Railway for the passenger service which ran into Newport High Street over the Western Valley lines from Bassaleg. The Taff Vale Railway provided the motive power for the mineral trains which ran over Pontypridd, Caerphilly & Newport metals to the junction with the Alexandra Dock Railway. In just over eighteen miles the passenger service to Pontypridd ran over five different companies: Great Western, Brecon & Merthyr, Rhymney, Pontypridd, Caerphilly & Newport and Taff Vale.

The Pontypridd, Caerphilly & Newport was absorbed by the Alexandra company in 1897. From 1 January 1899 the Newport to Pontypridd passenger service was worked by the Great Western Railway. In 1904 the Alexandra company bought two steam railmotors and started a service from a new station in Pontypridd, Tram Road, to Caerphilly. Seven very basic halts, without platforms, were provided along the route and difficulties must have been caused because the railmotors had no folding steps, only low straight steps at the rear. In 1910 the railmotors provided twelve return journeys a day, in addition to four daily Great Western trains to Newport. The railmotors did not last very long, being replaced by more conventional trains. From 1 January 1917 the Great Western service was suspended and the Alexandra trains were extended as far as Machen (on the Brecon & Merthyr) so that passengers could make a connection. The Alexandra Dock & Railway became part of the Great Western group in 1923.

Pontypridd Tram Road looking towards Pontypridd.

Treforest Halt, April 1952.

Dynea Halt, July 1956.

Groeswen Halt, July 1958.

Nantgarw Halt High Level, September 1952.

Barry Railway

Passenger service withdrawn	10 July 1930 (Tonteg Junction to Trehafod)
	10 September 1962 (Cadoxton to Treforest Junction)
Distance	16.7 miles (Cadoxton to Trehafod)
Company	Barry Dock & Railway

Stations closed	*Date of closure*
Pontypridd Graig *	10 July 1930
Treforest High Level **	10 July 1930
Tonteg Halt	10 September 1962
Efail Isaf ***	10 September 1962
Creigiau	10 September 1962
St-Y-Nyll Halt	November 1905
Wenvoe	10 September 1962

*   Known as Pontypridd until 1 July 1924.
**   Known as Treforest until 1 July 1924.
***   Also known as Efail Isaf & Llantwit Vardre.

The Barry Railway was a latecomer to the South Wales railway scene, being a result of the combination of mine owners' frustration at the delays on the Taff Vale Railway and with the Cardiff Docks (due to the volume of traffic) and their envy at the generous dividends paid by the Taff Vale. The Barry Dock & Railway was authorised in August 1884 with powers to build a dock and connecting lines up to the Rhondda with branches. The engineer was John Wolfe Barry and the docks took their name from him. The line from Tyn-y-caeau Junction to a junction with the Brecon & Merthyr at Barry Junction (and then by running powers on to Rhymney) was purely a mineral line. The company changed its name to the Barry Railway by Act of August 1891. The high demand for good quality coal ensured the line's success and in 1913 Barry exported almost one-third (over eleven million tons) of the total exported from South Wales. Dividends were also good at 10% between 1894 and 1897 while between 1913 and 1920 they were never less than $9\frac{1}{2}\%$.

In 1907 the Barry Railway was running its own steamer to holiday destinations in Devon and Somerset such as Minehead and Ilfracombe. Return fares from Cogan and stations to Barry Pier to Minehead or Weston-super-Mare were one shilling (five pence). However, the Act of 1904 enabling the Barry to operate ships was so restrictive that it sold its ships in 1909 but other companies called at Barry Pier until 1971.

Prior to the First World War and up to the beginning of 1917 there was a through train from Barry to Newcastle-on-Tyne using Great Western stock and Great Central stock on alternate days. The Barry insisted that its own locomotives be used between Barry and Cardiff and its favourite driver for the job was known as Ianto Full Pelt for reasons that can easily be guessed.

At the Grouping the company became a constituent of the Great Western group contributing 68 miles while the Vale of Glamorgan Railway, worked by the Barry, contributed a further 20.8 miles as a subsidiary company. The only part of the Barry system remaining open for passenger traffic is the Cogan to Barry line (including the line to Barry Island).

The main line was built from a junction with the Cogan to Barry line (which was the first section to open) at Cadoxton to a junction with the Taff Vale's Rhondda branch at Trehafod, from which point Barry passenger trains had running powers as far as Porth.

Although the line opened for mineral traffic on 13 May 1889 passenger services did not begin until March 1896. In 1910 there were only three daily trains from Barry to Porth with two on Sundays. However, there were also services from Cardiff Clarence Road via the South Wales main line to St Fagan's and around the loop to join the Barry line to Pontypridd. After 10 July 1930 trains to Porth joined the Taff Vale line at Treforest Junction and used the Taff Vale line to Porth.

Pontypridd Graig Station.

Pontypridd Graig Station, June 1922.

Auto-trailer w196w at Efail Isaf Station, July 1959.

Creigiau Station, July 1959.

2-4-2T No. 97 at Creigiau Sation, *c.* 1900.

Vale of Glamorgan Railway

Passenger service withdrawn	15 June 1964
Distance	19 miles (Bridgend to Barry)
Company	Vale of Glamorgan Railway

Stations closed	*Date of closure*
Southerndown Road	23 October 1961
Llandow Halt	15 June 1964
Llandow Wick Road Halt	15 June 1964
Llantwit Major	15 June 1964
St Athan *	15 June 1964
Gileston **	15 June 1964
Aberthaw ***	15 June 1964
Rhoose	15 June 1964

*   Known as St Athan Halt until 3 May 1943.
**   Sometimes known as Gileston for St Athan and the Leys.
***   Known as Aberthaw High Level between 1 July 1924 and 7 May 1945.

The Vale of Glamorgan Railway, strongly supported by the Barry Railway, was authorised in August 1889 with the intention, on the part of the Barry, to tap coal traffic from the Bridgend area while the colliery owners supported it as the port of Barry would then compete for their traffic with Swansea and Port Talbot.

The line opened from a junction west of Barry Town to a junction with the Great Western south of Bridgend (for passengers) and on to a junction on the Great Western Maesteg line at Coity for goods on 1 December 1897, and was worked by the Barry Railway from the start. Running powers to Tondu had been refused during the Bill's passage through Parliament so traffic for Barry Docks had to be exchanged at Coity Junction.

The line had two tunnels and a viaduct at Porthkerry Park but less than two months after opening part of this collapsed due to subsidence and a temporary diversion was used to the north for which Parliamentary powers were only obtained retrospectively. Despite being worked by the Barry Railway, the line remained independent until the Grouping. In 1910 there were 10 daily trains each way working to and from Cardiff although not all went through to Bridgend and several terminated at Llantwit Major. The line was kept for mineral traffic and has recently been reopened for passenger trains from Cardiff to Bridgend with intermediate stations at Rhoose (for Cardiff Airport) and Llantwit Major.

Southerdown Road Station, *c.* **1910.**

Llantwit Major Station, *c.* **1905.**

Railway Station, Llantwit Major, Glam. Nº 1391.

Gileston Station, *c.* **1905.**

Gileston Station for St. Athan. S1595 M

Aberthaw Station facing Barry, July 1959.

Rhoose Station.

Brecon & Merthyr Tydfil Junction Railway
Brecon & Merthyr Main Line *

Northern Division

Passenger service withdrawn	31 December 1962
Distance	25.9 miles (Northern Division: Brecon to Deri Junction)
Company	Brecon & Merthyr Tydfil Junction Railway

Stations closed	*Date of closure*
Pontsticill Junction	31 December 1962
Pant **	31 December 1962
Dowlais Top	31 December 1962
Pantywaun Halt	31 December 1962
Fochriw	31 December 1962
Ogilvie Colliery Platform ***	31 December 1962
Ogilvie Village Halt	31 December 1962

* The closed stations on this line that were in Brecknockshire were Brecon Free Street, Brecon Watton, Groesffordd Halt, Talyllyn (Brynderwen), Talyllyn Junction, Talybont-on Usk, Pentir Rhiw, Torpantau and Dolygaer.
** Known as Dowlais for Pant until May 1869.
*** Miners' halt; known as Ogilvie Colliery Halt until September 1928.

The Brecon & Abergavenny Canal opened in December 1811 but communications from Brecon to the industrial area around Merthyr Tydfil were difficult, there being a high ridge which formed a barrier to transport. The Brecon & Merthyr Tydfil Junction Railway was authorised as far as Talybont in August 1859 with the rest of the line being authorised in 1860 and 1862. However, besides linking the towns of its title (Merthyr having been reached by means of a branch) the line extended, by use of running powers, right into Newport. At the Grouping the Brecon & Merthyr became a subsidiary company, rather than a constituent, of the Great Western group.

The line opened from Brecon as far as Pant on 1 May 1863, and to Dowlais Top on 1 August 1867 from where it went on to an end-on junction with the Rhymney Railway at Deri Junction. Part of the trackbed, between Pant and Torpantau, now sees the narrow gauge trains of the Brecon Mountain Railway which has some interesting locomotives and is well worth seeing.

No. 9675 with the 1.19 p.m. for Merthyr, Pontsticill Junction Station, September 1951.

Pant Station, July 1958.

Dowlais Top Station facing Newport, July 1958.

Pantywaun Halt, July 1956.

Fochriw Station down platform, October 1952.

Merthyr Branch

Passenger service withdrawn	13 November 1961
Distance	6.8 miles (Pontsticill Junction to Merthyr)
Company	Brecon & Merthyr Tydfil Junction Railway

Stations closed	*Date of closure*
Pontsarn Halt *	13 November 1961
Cefn Coed **	13 November 1961
Heolgerrig Halt	13 November 1961

* Known as Pontsarn for Vaynor until 8 June 1953.
** Known as Cefn until 1 May 1920.

The Merthyr branch opened as far as Cefn on 1 August 1867 and to Merthyr exactly one year later. Although built by the Brecon & Merthyr the section from Morlais Junction to Rhydycar Junction became jointly owned with the London & North Western and it paid the Brecon & Merthyr £25,000 per mile for their share in the line. Most Brecon & Merthyr passengers for Merthyr had to change at Pontsticill although there were some through services between Brecon and Merthyr.

With the arrival of the London & North Western, Merthyr High Street Station (originally belonging to the Vale of Neath Railway) hosted five railway companies – Great Western, London & North Western, Taff Vale, Brecon & Merthyr, Rhymney – each with their own booking office. The station was the scene of an accident in May 1874 when the couplings parted between two wagons of a Vale of Neath goods train climbing through Merthyr Tunnel and seventeen wagons hurtled down the gradient into Merthyr Station and a Brecon & Merthyr passenger train, smashing several coaches and pushing the loco, an 0-6-0 named 'Elephant', through the wall and several feet into the town's John Street. One person died and about 50 were injured.

Cefn Coed Station facing Merthyr, September 1957.

Dowlais Branch

Passenger service withdrawn 2 May 1960
Distance 1.4 miles (Pant Junction to Dowlais)
Company Brecon & Merthyr Tydfil Junction Railway

Stations closed *Date of closure*
Dowlais Central* 2 May 1960

* Known as Dowlais until 1 July 1924.

The branch to Dowlais opened on 23 June 1869. The junction for the branch was north of Pant, where passengers changed, so trains had to reverse both going on to the branch and coming off it. Services were well planned with a train leaving Dowlais to meet an arriving main-line train and then return to Dowlais. In this way the station saw a total of sixteen arrivals and departures on a weekday in 1910.

Pant Station's Dowlais Branch platform, November 1957.

Pantysgallog Halt facing Dowlais Central, November 1957.

Dowlais Central Station, November 1957.

Caerphilly to Machen

Passenger service withdrawn	17 September 1956
Distance	3.9 miles (East Branch Junction to Machen Junction)
Company	Rumney Tramroad
	Brecon & Merthyr Tydfil Junction Railway
	Pontypridd Caerphilly & Newport Railway

Stations closed	*Date of closure*
Gwernydomen Halt	17 September 1956
Fountain Bridge Halt	17 September 1956
Waterloo Halt	17 September 1956
White Hart Halt	30 June 1952

When the Rumney Tramroad gained powers to convert to a railway it also gained powers for a branch from Machen to Caerphilly. By the time it was opened in 1865 the Rumney had been acquired by the Brecon & Merthyr. As built, there was a very sharp gradient of 1 in 39 going towards Machen and this severely restricted the weight of (generally loaded) trains that could be worked in that direction. To overcome this, the Pontypridd, Caerphilly & Newport Railway proposed and built the Machen loop to the north with a gradient of only 1 in 200. This was later transferred to the Brecon & Merthyr in return for 50% of the earnings of the Machen to Caerphilly line. Traffic to Newport then used the northern line while up trains (from Newport) used the southern line. Only down trains called at Fountain Bridge Halt, on the northern loop, and only up trains called at Waterloo Halt on the south loop. White Hart Halt had platforms on each line divided by a main road. Passenger services were worked for some time by the Great Western running the service between Pontypridd and Newport. This was temporarily withdrawn in January 1917 and then the Alexandra Dock & Railway extended its Pontypridd to Caerphilly service as far as Machen.

Gwernydomen Halt, April 1957.

Cardiff Railway

Passenger service withdrawn	20 July 1931 (north of Coryton)
Distance	10.8 miles (Cardiff to Rhydyfelin)
Company	Cardiff Railway

Stations closed	*Date of closure*
Tongwynlais	20 July 1931
Glanyllyn	20 July 1931
Nantgarw Halt Low Level *	20 July 1931
Upper Boat	20 July 1931
Rhydyfelin Low Level Halt **	20 July 1931

*   Known as Nantgarw until 1 July 1924.
**   Known as Rhydyfelin until 1 July 1924.

The Bute Docks Company, owners of Cardiff's Bute Docks, felt they would be in a better position if they had their own railway to bring coal to these. There were attempts to merge with existing railway companies including both the Rhymney and the Taff Vale, but an Act of 1897 authorised a change of name to the Cardiff Railway and the construction of more than 20 miles of railway. In the event only the section from a junction with the Rhymney Railway at Heath to Treforest was built. At Treforest Junction three railways already made connection to the Taff Vale main line – it was claimed that there were 450 movements a day over that and the Cardiff Railway had another junction authorised. This required the construction of the Treforest viaduct and on 15 May 1909 the first goods train, with the Marquis of Bute on the footplate, crossed the viaduct (passenger services began on 1 March 1911). The Taff Vale shut the new junction authorised by the Cardiff Railway, claiming it had been built in the wrong place and there was a lot of legal argument over it which came to nothing. In 1917 E.A. Prosser, the general manager of the Rhymney, became general manager of the Taff Vale and Cardiff companies as well and that led to a less argumentative atmosphere. The viaduct was demolished in the Second World War when the steel was needed elsewhere.

The Cardiff Railway began its own passenger service in March 1911 using railmotors bought from the Gloucester Carriage & Wagon Company. Two coach units were bought and three locomotives (sub-contracted to Sissons of Gloucester as Gloucester Carriage & Wagon did not build engine units) plus a further two trailers. Seating was provided for both first and third classes (second class was not provided; it had already been abolished by some companies).

In 1922 there were eight daily return services and four on Sundays. At the grouping the Cardiff Railway became part of the Great Western group and passenger services north of Coryton were withdrawn although services still run to Coryton, a distance of about five miles from Cardiff.

Cardiff Railway railcar at Rhydyfelin Station on the first day of passenger service, 1 March 1911.

Neath to Pontypool

This line was built as two separate sections and, originally, even to two separate gauges. The Taff Vale Extension Railway of the Newport, Abergavenny & Hereford Railway came from the east and the Vale of Neath Railway from the west to meet in the Aberdare Valley.

Taff Vale Extension Railway *

Passenger service withdrawn	15 June 1964
Distance	20.8 miles (Pontypool to Middle Duffryn)
Company	Newport, Abergavenny & Hereford Railway

Stations closed	*Date of closure*
Hengoed High Level **	15 June 1964
Llancaiach ***	1 July 1912
Nelson & Llancaiach	15 June 1964
Treharris	15 June 1964
Trelewis Halt	15 June 1964
Quaker's Yard High Level ****	15 June 1964
Penrhiwceiber High Level *****	15 June 1964
Mountain Ash Cardiff Road †	15 June 1964
Duffryn Crossing Halt	2 April 1917

* Closed stations on this line that were in Monmouthshire were Pontypool Clarence Street, Cefn Crib, Crumlin Valley, Colliery Platform, Hafodyrynys Platform, Crumlin, Crumlin High Level, Treowen Halt, Pentwynmawr Platform, Penar Junction Halt and Pontllanffraith Low Level.

** Known as Rhymney Junction until 1 July 1906 and then as Hengoed & Maesycwmmer until 1 July 1924.

*** Known as Llancaiach & Nelson until 1902; closed on the opening of Nelson & Llancaiach to the west.

**** Known as Quaker's Yard until 1894.

***** Known as Penrhiwceiber until 1 July 1924.

† Known as Mountain Ash until 1 July 1924.

The Taff Vale Extension Railway (from Pontypool Road to a junction with the Taff Vale Railway at Quaker's Yard) of the Newport, Abergavenny & Hereford Railway was authorised as a standard gauge line in 1846. Once the Crumlin viaduct was ready (probably the largest in the world at the time at 1,650 feet long with a maximum height of 200 feet), it opened as far as Pontllanfraith on 1 June 1857 and on to Quaker's Yard (Low Level) on 11 January 1858. There, it provided the Taff Vale Railway with its first link to another railway of the same gauge so that Quaker's Yard became a very busy interchange point.

Parliamentary approval for an extension to link with the Vale of Neath at Middle Duffryn was obtained in 1857 but in case the Neath line retained the broad gauge it also gained powers to join the Taff Vale at Mountain Ash and use its lines to Aberdare. The extension did not open for freight until January 1864, eventually opening for passengers in October the same year. The Newport, Abergavenny & Hereford Railway became part of the West Midland Railway when that company was formed on 14 June 1860; the West Midland itself was absorbed by the Great Western on 1 August 1863.

Hengoed High Level Station, July 1958.

The old Llancaiach Station, closed in 1912, *c.* **1900.**

Nelson & Llancaiach Station, 1912.

No. 5624 with the 6.15 p.m train from Cardiff to Aberdare at Nelson & Llanciach Station, July 1959.

Great Western auto-trailer No. 91 at Treharris Station, *c.* 1910.

Trelewis Halt, July 1958.

Quaker's Yard Station facing Pontypool Road, November 1957.

Quaker's Yard Station, *c.* 1905.

The same view as above in July 1959.

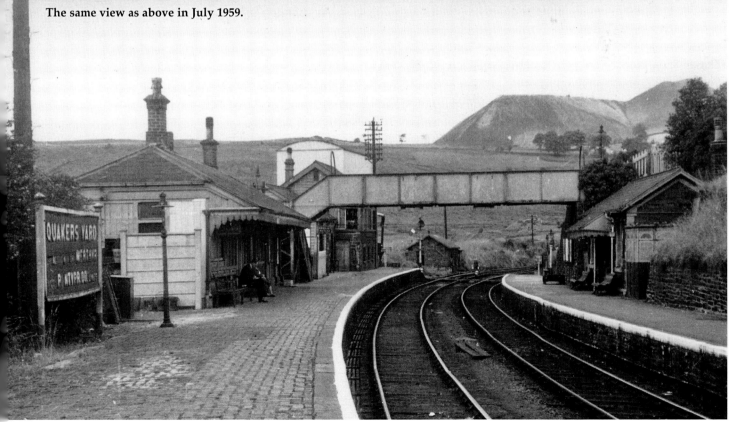

Vale of Neath Railway

Passenger service withdrawn	15 June 1964
Distance	20.9 miles (Middle Duffryn to Neath Junction)
Company	Vale of Neath Railway

Stations closed	*Date of closure*
Middle Duffryn Colliery *	15 June 1964
Cwmbach Halt	15 June 1964
Cwmbach Colliery	closure date unknown
Aberdare High Level **	15 June 1964
Trecynon Halt	15 June 1964
Merthyr Road	2 November 1853
Hirwaun ***	15 June 1964
Rhigos Halt	15 June 1964
Pontwalby Halt	15 June 1964
British Rhondda Halt	1 May 1911
Cwmrhyd-Y-Gau Halt ****	by October 1945
Glyn Neath	15 June 1964
Resolven	15 June 1964
Melyncourt Halt	15 June 1964
Clyne Halt	15 June 1964
Aberdilais Halt *****	15 June 1964

*	Miners' halt.
**	Known as Aberdare until 1 July 1924.
***	Known as Hirwain until September 1928.
****	Workmen's halt.
*****	Known as Aberdylais until 7 June 1954

The Vale of Neath Railway was incorporated in August 1846 to build a line from Neath to Gelly Tarw Junction where the line branched, the northern one going towards Merthyr Tydfil and the southern one to Aberdare. The line was heavily influenced by the South Wales Railway, with which it made a connection, its engineer was Brunel, and it was built to the broad gauge. The Aberdare line opened first on 24 September 1851.

The Aberdare Valley Railway was built with Vale of Neath support and opened to Middle Duffryn in November 1856. It was absorbed by the Vale of Neath in 1864 having always been worked by it. A third rail was laid during 1863 so that standard gauge trains could run through from Pontypool to Neath. The Great Western absorbed the Vale of Neath line on 1 February 1865.

The connection with the Taff Vale Extension enabled standard gauge goods trains to run through to Swansea and both the Great Western and the London & North Western provided such a service. Great Western passenger trains ran through to Swansea from Hereford and Birmingham.

Cwmbach Halt, July 1959.

Hirwain Station, *c.* 1910.

Pontwalby Halt, July 1956.

Glyn Neath Station looking towards Hirwain, August 1949.

Resolven Station, *c.* 1910.

Aberdilais Halt, July 1956.

Cwmaman Colliery Branch

Passenger service withdrawn	22nd September 1924
Distance	5.4 miles (Gelly Tarw Junction to Cwmaman Colliery)
Company	Vale of Neath Railway

Stations closed	*Date of closure*
Black Lion Crossing Halt *	*c.* 1932
Ton Llwyd Halt	2 January 1922
Godreaman Halt **	*c.* 1932
Cwmneol Halt	22 September 1924
Cwmaman Crossing Halt	22 September 1924
Cwmaman Colliery Halt ***	*c.* 1932

*   Known as Black Lion Crossing until 22 September 1924 after which date it was used only by miners.

**   This station replaced an earlier one of the same name on 2 January 1922 and after 22 September 1924 was used only by miners.

*** Used only by miners after 22 September 1924.

This was one of two mineral branches built from Gelly Tarw Junction and splitting at Dare Junction, being open for mineral traffic by 1857. The Great Western began a railmotor service between Black Lion Crossing and Cwmaman Colliery, a distance of about two and three quarter miles, in 1906. In 1910 there were eight daily trains each way with an additional four on Saturdays and in 1922 ten in each direction.

Cwmaman Colliery Halt the colliery is on the right.

Merthyr Branch

Passenger service withdrawn	31 December 1962
Distance	6.4 miles (Gelly Tarw Junction to Merthyr)
Company	Vale of Neath Railway

Stations closed	*Date of closure*
Llwydcoed	31 December 1962
Abernant	31 December 1962

Opening of the line to Merthyr was delayed by the construction of the 2,495-yard-long Merthyr tunnel which had been started in 1847 but was not finished until 1853. Even by then the Merthyr terminus was not finished and the line did not open until 2 November 1853. Mixed gauge tracks reached Merthyr but not into the station until 1867. In 1887 there were four daily trains and two on Sundays and by 1910 there were eight daily trains. The Vale of Neath station in Merthyr remains open for trains using the old Taff Vale line.

Swansea & Neath Railway

Passenger service withdrawn	28 September 1936
Distance	7.8 miles (Neath Junction to Wind Street Junction)
Company	Swansea & Neath Railway

Stations closed	*Date of closure*
Neath Riverside *	15 June 1964
Neath Abbey **	28 September 1936
Cardonnel Halt	28 September 1936
Cape Platform ***	11 September 1933
Briton Ferry Road **	28 September 1936
Swansea Wind Street	1 March 1873
Swansea East Dock ****	28 September 1936

*   Known as Neath Bridge Street until 17 September 1926 and as Neath Low Level until
       1 July 1924.
**   Closed between 1 March 1873 and October 1880.
***   Workmen's platform.
**** This station, on the east side of the Tawe, replaced Wind Street on the west side.

The Vale of Neath's junction with the South Wales Railway at Neath faced towards Cardiff although most traffic went to Swansea by the steeply graded and rather indirect South Wales line. The Swansea & Neath Railway was originally proposed in 1861 as an independent line linking these two places along the coast. After the Great Western and the South Wales got involved the Neath Harbour Commissioners and the Vale of Neath both opposed it in the Commons. As their opposition was successful both the large companies lost interest and the bill went to the Lords with Vale of Neath support. The Vale of Neath was allowed to provide the majority of the capital and in 1863 took the line over; the line opened, as a mixed gauge line, to passengers on 15 July that year. On 29 November 1865 it was the scene of a very serious accident involving the telescopic bridge at North Dock when a locomotive and 30 coal wagons plunged through the open bridge with fatal consequences.

Rail motor No. 37 at Neath Riverside Station, *c.* 1910.

Neath Riverside Station, *c.* 1910.

Neath Riverside Station, July 1959.

Neath Riverside Station, April 1961.

Neath Abbey, March 1949.

Briton Ferry Road Station.

Swansea East Dock Station, July 1956.

Heads of the Valleys Line *

Passenger service withdrawn	6 January 1958
Distance	24.5 miles (Abergavenny Junction to Merthyr High Street)
Company	Merthyr, Tredegar & Abergavenny Railway

Stations closed	*Date of closure*
Rhymney Bridge	6 January 1958
Dowlais High Street **	6 January 1958
Pontsarn ***	13 November 1961
Cefn Coed ****	13 November 1961

*	Closed stations on this line that were in Brecknockshire were Gilwern Halt, Clydach, Gelli Felen Halt and Brynmawr; closed stations in Monmouthshire were Govilon, Beaufort, Trevil Halt and Nantybwch.
**	Known as Dowlais until April 1891.
***	Known as Pontsarn for Vaynot until 8 June 1853.
****	Known as Cefn until 1 May 1920.

There were a number of tramroads extending westwards from the Brecon & Abergavenny Canal and one of these, Bailey's Tramroad, which was built to the unusual gauge of four feet four inches, formed the basis of the Merthyr, Tredegar & Abergavenny Railway. That scheme had succeeded over the rival Breconshire Railway & Canal Company and was authorised in August 1859. The same Act transferred to the Merthyr, Tredegar & Abergavenny the section of the three-feet-six-inch-gauge Llanvihangel Railway between the canal wharf at Govilon and the intended junction with the Newport, Abergavenny & Hereford Railway east of Abergavenny.

The line formed an important part of London & North Western strategy to gain access to South Wales industries. Having failed to gain outright control of the Newport, Abergavenny & Hereford or the Shrewsbury & Hereford, the London & North Western, by being joint lessees of the Shrewsbury & Hereford, was left with running powers over the Newport, Abergavenny & Hereford and so gained access to Abergavenny. Before the Merthyr, Tredegar & Abergavenny was opened the London & North Western reached an agreement to lease the line for 1,000 years in the face of opposition from the West Midland Railway. The London & North Western absorbed the Merthyr, Tredegar & Abergavenny on 30 June 1866. Passenger services began as far as Brynmawr on 1 October 1862 (although this was preceded by a ceremonial opening on 29 September). The line was extended as far as Nantybwch on 1 March 1864.

Despite strong opposition from the Brecon & Merthyr Railway the line was extended jointly with the Rhymney Railway to Rhymney Bridge on 5 September 1871 and opened on 1 January 1873 to Ivor Junction with the Brecon and Merthyr's Dowlais line. Access to Merthyr was gained over the Brecon & Merthyr branch, which had opened in 1868, and became a joint line when the London & North Western paid half the construction cost. The final expensive link between Penywern Junction and Morlais Junction, which included the 574-yard-long Morlais tunnel, was opened on 1 June 1879.

The line was doubled in 1877 and the London & North Western gained access to Cardiff by running powers over the Rhymney Railway. Goods traffic developed so much that the London & North Western opened its own goods depot in the Cardiff Docks district while through coaches were run between Cardiff and Crewe, Manchester and Liverpool. These through services lasted until the First World War.

The onset of the Great Depression brought a rationalisation of goods services with the Great Western and the London Midland Scottish (which had taken over the London & North Western) working more closely. London Midland Scottish goods traffic for Cardiff was sent via Newport, thus removing the need to work it along the steep gradients of the Merthyr, Tredegar & Abergavenny. Amongst other steep gradients along the route was over five miles at 1 in 37 to 40 between Govilon and Brynmawr. Remaining goods services were withdrawn on 22 November 1954.

For many years the line was the haunt of London & North Western 0-6-2Ts (Coal Tanks) and almost 50 of them were shedded at Abergavenny, although freight services were worked by Beames 0-8-4Ts and later by 0-8-0s. In the 1950s various Great Western tanks worked the line as it became part of the Western Region at Nationalisation.

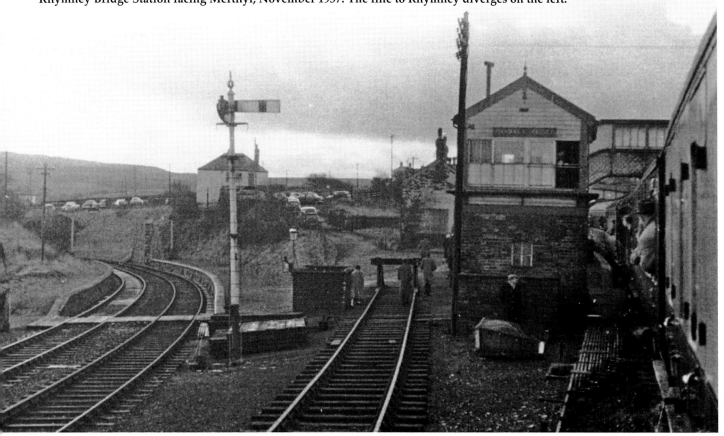

Rhymney Bridge Station facing Merthyr, November 1957. The line to Rhymney diverges on the left.

Dowlais High Street Station, January 1958.

Llynvi & Ogmore Railway

The Llynvi & Ogmore Railway had its origins in two earlier railways, the Llynvi Valley Railway and the Ogmore Valley Railway. The Llynvi Valley Railway bought two earlier tramroads, the Duffryn, Llynvi & Porthcawl Railway and the Bridgend Railway, which joined the Duffryn west of Tondu. The Llynvi was authorised as a broad gauge railway and built only partly on the trackbed of the earlier tramroads. It opened for mineral traffic in August 1861 and for passengers between Bridgend (where it made a junction with the South Wales Railway) and Maesteg in February 1864 and to Porthcawl in August 1865.

The Ogmore Valley Railway was authorised in July 1863 as a standard gauge line from Nantymoel to a junction with the Llynvi at Tondu and thence to Porthcawl by means of a third rail. After promoting a joint bill for the improvement of Porthcawl harbour the two companies agreed to amalgamate and the Llynvi & Ogmore was formed on 1 July 1866. The enlarged company decided to use the standard gauge and this was in use throughout the line by 1868 although the broad gauge rails remained in place (so that Great Western broad gauge wagons could still be used although hauled by standard gauge locos) until the Great Western converted its lines in South Wales in 1872. The system was completed by the Cardiff & Ogmore Railway, which opened in October 1876, and its link to Tondu (Bryncethin Junction to Tynycoed Junction), but neither of these lines had passenger stations so are not detailed here.

The Llynvi & Ogmore had its workshops at Tondu and there was a large shed with almost 50 locomotives being stabled there after the Second World War. On 1 July 1873 the Great Western took over working the Llynvi & Ogmore with full amalgamation ten years later.

Bridgend to Abergwynfi

Passenger service withdrawn	13 June 1960 (Abergwynfi to Cymmer Afan (Gelli))
	26 February 1968 (Cymmer Afan (Gelli) to Cymmer Afan (East Junction))
	22 June 1970 (Cymmer Afan (East Junction) to Bridgend)
Distance	15.4 miles (Bridgend to Abergwynfi)
Company	Llynvi Valley Railway / Great Western Railway

Stations closed	*Date of closure*
Bridgend *	1 July 1873
Llangynwyd **	15 July 1970
Troedyrhiew Garth	15 July 1970
Maesteg ***	15 July 1970
Nantyffyllon ****	15 July 1970
Caerau	15 July 1970
Cymmer Afan *****	15 July 1970
Abergwynfi	13 June 1960

*   After this date trains used the South Wales main line station.
**   Known as Llangonoyd until March 1935, closed between 1 January 1917 and 1 January 1919.
*** Known as Maesteg Castle Street until May 1968 and as Maesteg until 1 July 1924.
**** Known as Tywith until 1 January 1903.
***** Known as Cymmer General until January 1950 when it was amalgamated with and renamed Cymmer Afan. Known as Cymmer for Glyncorrwg until 1 July 1924.

The line was extended north from Nantyffyllon to Abergwynfi for minerals in July 1878 and opened for passengers as far as Cymmer two years later and to Abergwynfi in March 1886. At Abergwynfi the Great Western Railway had its own colliery to supply locomotive coal and the Avon Colliery was sunk in 1877 for that purpose. The original power for the pit winder was an old locomotive named 'Alexander'. The pit remained in railway ownership until 1912. At Cymmer there were three railway stations for the Llynvi & Ogmore, the Rhondda & Swansea Bay and the South Wales Mineral railways. In 1910 there were only four daily trains between Bridgend and Abergwynfi but an extra eight were provided on Saturdays. This line was reopened as far as Maesteg in 1992 with trains running from Cardiff Central.

LLangynwyd Station, July 1959.

Troedyrhiew Garth Station, July 1959.

Maesteg (Castle Street) Station, May 1960.

Caerau Station, c. 1910.

Cymmer General, in 1949, before it was renamed Cymmer Afan.

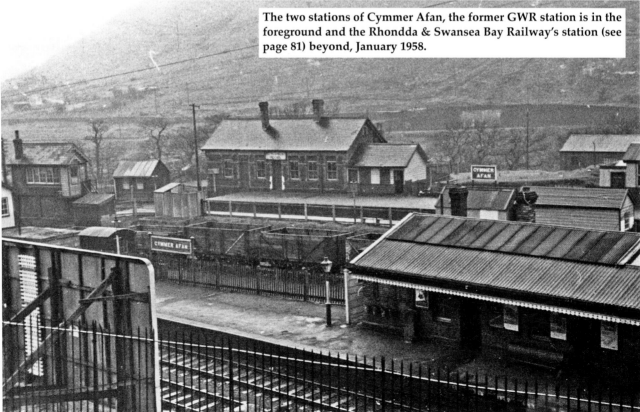

The two stations of Cymmer Afan, the former GWR station is in the foreground and the Rhondda & Swansea Bay Railway's station (see page 81) beyond, January 1958.

Abergwynfi Station, November 1957.

Abergwynfi Station, November 1957.

Porthcawl Branch

Passenger service withdrawn	9 September 1963
Distance	9.7 miles (Tondu to Porthcawl Harbour)
Company	Llynvi Valley Railway

Stations closed	*Date of closure*
Kenfig Hill *	5 May 1958
Pyle **	13 November 1876
Nottage Halt ***	9 September 1963
Porthcawl ****	9 September 1963

*   Known as Cefn until 1 August 1885.

**   Earlier known as Tydraw, it was amalgamated with the Great Western station on 13 November 1876.

*** Known as Porthcawl Golfers' Platform until 14 July 1924.

**** This station replaced an earlier station to the north on 1 March 1916.

A connection between the Porthcawl line and the South Wales main line was provided at Pyle in November 1876. Another link, the Pyle West Loop, was provided in September 1946 and removed the need for traffic between Porthcawl, Swansea and Port Talbot to reverse at Pyle. Porthcawl docks fell into disuse towards the end of the nineteenth century and closed in 1898 when they were filled in to provide an esplanade and, later, a car park. In 1887 there were four daily trains to Porthcawl with simultaneous departures from Tondu for the Porthcawl and Abergwynfi lines. By 1910, while four daily trains still worked through from Tondu, there were an additional nine trains between the main line at Pyle and Porthcawl.

Pyle Station, *c.* 1910.

Kenfig Hill, *c.* 1905.

Nottage Halt, March 1949.

Locomotive No. 4404 with 10.50 a.m. from Pyle at Porthcawl Station, September 1957.

Porthcawl Station before it was rebuilt in 1916, *c.* **1900.**

Porthcawl Station after it was rebuilt, August 1948.

Ogmore Valley Railway

Passenger service withdrawn	5 May 1958
Distance	7.1 miles (Nantymoel to Tondu Junction)
Company	Ogmore Valley Railway

Stations closed	*Date of closure*
Nantymoel	5 May 1958
Wyndham Halt	5 May 1958
Ogmore Vale *	5 May 1958
Lewistown Halt	4 June 1951
Blackmill	5 May 1958
Brynmenyn	5 May 1958

*   Known as Tynewydd Ogmore Vale until 1 January 1902.

This line opened on 1 August 1865. Much of the line rose at 1 in 41 with a final stretch of 1 in 27. It carried considerable coal traffic from Wyndham, Western and Penllwyngwen collieries. In 1910 there were six daily trains from Bridgend to Nantymoel.

Nantymoel Station, *c.* **1905.**

Brynmenyn Station, *c.* **1905.**

Ely Valley Extension Railway

Passenger service withdrawn	22 September 1930
Distance	2.5 miles (Gellyrhaidd to Gilfach Goch)
Company	Ely Valley Extension Railway

Stations closed	*Date of closure*
Gilfach Goch *	22 September 1930
Hendreforgan **	22 September 1930

* Known as Gilfach until 30 June 1928; closed between 5 March and 26 March 1928.
** Closed between 5 March and 26 March 1928.

The Ogmore Valley had visions of linking with the Taff Vale and Rhymney companies and as part of these aspirations absorbed the Ely Valley Extension Railway in July 1865. This had been authorised in 1863 as a broad gauge line from the Gellyrhaidd line of the Ely Valley Railway to Gilfach Goch. Despite being absorbed by the standard gauge Ogmore Valley in July 1865, with which it had at that time no physical connection, the line was worked by the Great Western as part of the Ely Valley Railway. It opened on 16 October 1865. Besides the public service, miners were carried as far as Gilfach Goch Colliery and the line remained open for workmen until the 1950s and mineral traffic until June 1961.

Gilfach Goch Station, *c.* **1910.**

Hendreforgan Station, *c.* 1900.

Black Mill to Hendreforgan

Passenger service withdrawn	22 September 1930
Distance	3.4 miles
Company	Llynvi & Ogmore Railway

This line was built to link the Ely Valley Extension line with the rest of the Llynvi & Ogmore system and opened on 1 September 1875. After that services ran from Black Mill, on the Ogmore Valley line, to Gilfach Goch and there were four trains between those places in 1887. There were no stations on this stretch of line.

Great Western Railway: Garw Branch

Passenger service withdrawn	9 February 1953
Distance	5.7 miles (Brynmenyn Junction to Blaengarw)
Company	Great Western Railway

Stations closed	*Date of closure*
Blaengarw	9 February 1953
Pontycymmer	9 February 1953
Pontyrhyll	9 February 1953
Llangeinor *	9 February 1953

*   Closed between 1 January 1917 and 1 January 1919.

This line opened from a junction near Tondu on 25 October 1876 but was a mineral line only until August 1887 when a passenger service as far as Pontyrhyll began. At that time there were seven daily trains between Brynmenyn and Pontyrhyll, although Pontycymmer is in the timetable with no service shown. The passenger service was extended to Blaengarw on 1 May 1902. By 1910 there were six daily trains between Brynmenyn and Blaengarw, with the Port Talbot adding an additional five from Port Talbot to Pontyrhyll and Blaengarw. While the maximum gradient was 'only' 1 in 34 along the passenger section, it increased to 1 in 18 beyond that.

Blaengarw Station, *c.* 1910.

Blaengarw Station, July 1959.

Pontycymmer Station, July 1959.

Staggered platforms at Pontyrhyll Station, *c.* 1910.

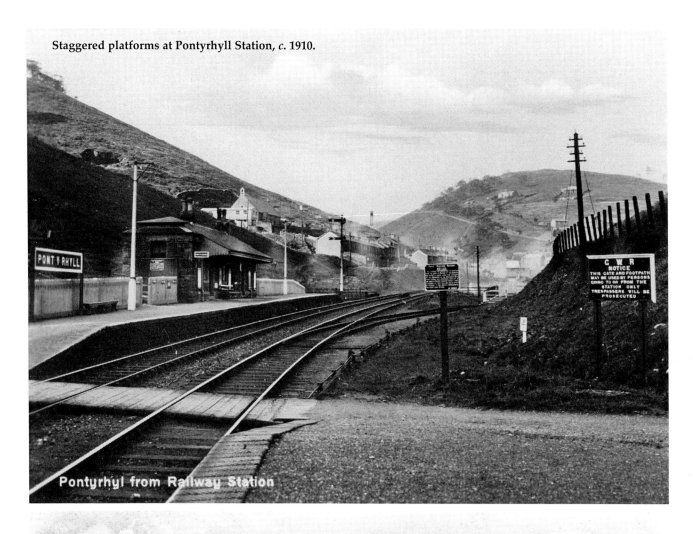

Llangeinor Station looking towards the village.

Ely Valley Railway

Although never part of the Llynvi & Ogmore it is convenient to include this railway here as it connected with the Llynvi & Ogmore and was in the same area. The Ely Valley Railway was authorised as a broad gauge line in July 1857 and built a network of lines from a junction with the South Wales Railway at Llantrisant. In 1860 the company promoted a bill to convert to standard gauge and build a line to Cardiff, although it was never actually built, being merely a ploy to persuade the Great Western to convert its broad gauge lines. The system was always worked by the Great Western, initially under lease, and was only absorbed in 1903.

Penygraig Branch

Passenger service withdrawn	9 June 1958
Distance	7.1 miles (Llantrisant to Penygraig)
	1.9 miles (Penygraig to Blaen)Clydach)
Company	Ely Valley Railway / Ely & Clydach Valleys Railway

Stations closed	*Date of closure*
Clydach Vale Platform *	closed by September 1926
Penygraig **	9 June 1958
Tonyrefail	9 June 1958
Coed Ely	9 June 1958

*   Miners' platform.
**   Known as Penygraig & Tonypandy between 12 July 1911 and 13 July 1925.

This line opened as far as Tonyrefail on 2 August 1860 and was extended to Penygraig in December 1862. It was extended to the mines at Blaenclydach on 10 August 1878 by the Ely & Clydach Valleys Railway which became part of the Great Western in 1880. The passenger service began on 1 May 1901 and in 1910 there were seven daily trains between Llantrisant and Penygraig.

Penygraig Station, January 1958.

Tonyrefail Station, c. 1910.

Tonyrefail Station, January 1958.

Brofiskin Branch

Passenger service withdrawn   31 March 1952
Distance   2.8 miles (Mwyndy to Brofiskin)
Company   Ely Valley Railway

This line opened on 8 January 1862. There were no stations and the only passenger service over it was by virtue of the Taff Vale's running powers for its service from Pontypridd via Llantrisant to Aberthaw.

Gellyrhaidd Branch

Distance   1.3 miles (Gellyrhaidd Branch)
Company   Ely Valley Railway

This line opened on 8 January 1862. There were no stations or passenger service but it provided the start point for the Ely Valley Extension line.

London & North Western Railway to Swansea

Passenger service withdrawn	15 June 1964
Distance	12.3 miles (Pontardulais to Swansea Victoria)
Company	Llanelly Railway

Stations closed	*Date of closure*
Grovesend	6 June 1932
Gorseinon	15 June 1964
Gowerton South *	15 June 1964
Dunvant	15 June 1964
Killay	15 June 1964
Mumbles Road	15 June 1964
Swansea Bay **	15 June 1964
Swansea Victoria	15 June 1964

*   Known as Gower Road until 8 June 1886 and as Gowerton until January 1950.
**   This station replaced an earlier one of the same name 400 metres east on 2 June 1892.

Powers were granted to the Llanelly Railway in 1861 for a line from its existing line at Pontardulais to Swansea with a branch to Penclawdd. At the same time it also obtained powers for a line from Llandilo to Abergwili and so to Carmarthen. The line to Swansea opened for goods in January 1866 but not to passengers until 14 December 1867. The Llanelly had taken a lease on the Vale of Towy Railway north from Llandilo to Llandovery where it would meet the London & North Western's Central Wales line. The London & North Western had its sights firmly set on Swansea and the rich traffic the port could bring so when the Llanelly's lease of the Vale of Towy expired a new joint lease was agreed with the Llanelly and the London & North Western. The Llanelly granted running powers to the London & North Western which gave it access to Swansea as well as Llanelly and Carmarthen (and, by running powers, beyond to Pembroke Dock). By the time the London & North Western opened its Llandovery line on 8 June 1868 powers were in place for services through to Swansea.

In 1871 the Swansea and Carmarthen lines of the Llanelly were made a separate company, known as the Swansea & Carmarthen Railway, and were worked by the London & North Western from July that year. It became part of the larger company in September 1873. The line enabled the London & North Western to provide a fairly direct route from southwest Wales to the north and there were also through services from Euston. In 1887 the 10 a.m. from Euston got to Swansea Victoria at 7.35 p.m., covering a distance of 278.3 miles via Shrewsbury; by 1910 the same train did not arrive until 7.55 p.m.

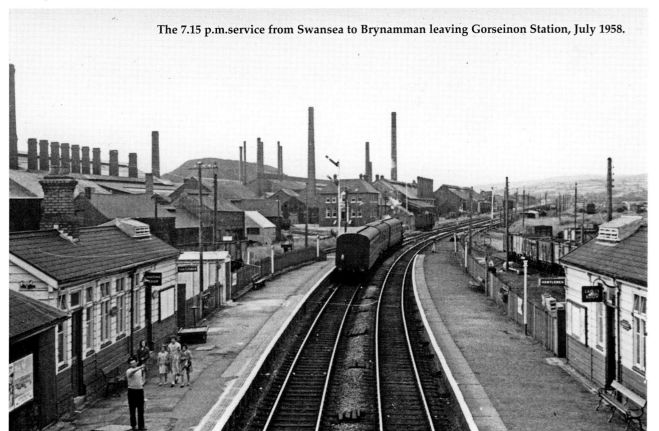

The 7.15 p.m. service from Swansea to Brynamman leaving Gorseinon Station, July 1958.

Gowerton Station, *c.* 1910.

Gowerton Station, *c.* 1910.

Killay Station.

Mumbles Road Station is just visible among the trees on the left. The Mumbles & Swansea railway runs under the bridge.

Mumbles Road Station, May 1959.

Swansea Bay Station, September 1957.

Swansea Victoria.

Penclawdd Branch

Passenger service withdrawn	5 January 1931
Distance	4.8 miles
Company	Llanelly Railway / London & North Western Railway

Stations closed	*Date of closure*
Penclawdd	5 January 1931
Llanmorlais	5 January 1931

The Penclawdd Branch made a junction with the Llanelly's Swansea line at Gowerton and opened for passengers on 14 December 1867, although it is likely it opened for goods about August 1865. The London & North Western obtained powers for the extension to Llanmorlais in 1874 and this opened for goods in 1877, but passengers had to walk or use a horse bus until the new terminus opened on 1 March 1884.

Penclawdd Station, *c.* **1910.**

Midland Railway to Swansea

Passenger service withdrawn	25 September 1950
Distance	19 miles
Company	Swansea Vale Railway

Stations closed	*Date of closure*
Brynamman East *	25 September 1950
Cwmllynfel **	25 September 1950
Gwys	25 September 1950
Cwmtwrch Well Halt	25 September 1950
Ystalyfera	25 September 1950
Ynysygeinon	1 March 1862
Pontardawe	25 September 1950
Glais ***	25 September 1950
Birchgrove ****	1 March 1875
Clydach-on-Tawe South *****	25 September 1950
Morriston East †	25 September 1950
Upper Bank	25 September 1950
Swansea St Thomas ††	25 September 1950

*	Known as Brynamman until 1 January 1950.
**	Known as Gwaun-cae-Gurwen Colliery Halt until 1 July 1909.
***	This station replaced the earlier Swansea Vale station on the same site.
****	This station lay on the original line and closed when all passenger services took the Morriston loop.
*****	Known as Cwm Clydach until 1 November 1901 and then Clydach-on-Tawe until 1 January 1950.
†	Known as Morriston until 1 January 1950.
††	Originally known as Swansea the date of the change of name is uncertain but Bradshaw calls it St Thomas by 1887 although this could be unofficial.

The Swansea Vale Railway began life as a collection of tramroads extending up the east bank of the River Tawe from Swansea. After an early attempt to extend the line to Pontardawe was unsuccessful attempts were made to sell the line to the South Wales Railway, but these also failed. It opened from Swansea to Glais in 1852 and in 1855 obtained powers to extend to Brynamman, opening to Pontardawe in February 1860 and to Brynamman in January 1864. To serve the new suburb of Morriston and industries in the area a loop was built between 1871 and 1873 from Upper Bank to Glais Junction and all passenger services were sent that way with the stations on the loop (Cwm Clydach and Morriston) opening on 1 March 1875.

The Midland Railway wanted some of the rich pickings to be had in South Wales and it got there by taking over one line, the Hereford, Hay & Brecon (having already used running powers over another line, the Great Western, to get to Hereford), and then using running powers over two other lines, the Cambrian and the Brecon & Merthyr, to reach Brecon. The final link in the strategy fell into place when the Swansea Vale and Neath & Brecon Junction Railway opened in 1873, making a junction with the Swansea Vale at Ynys-y-Geinon. Under the SV&NBJ's original Act the Swansea Vale had obtained running powers through to Brecon over the Neath & Brecon, thus the Midland saw an opportunity and took a lease on the Swansea Vale in 1874 and took it over completely in August 1876 gaining the running powers, now over three other companies, at the same time.

Through coaches between Birmingham and Swansea started to run in 1877. There were two distinct services: suburban services to Brynamman (in 1910 there were eleven daily trains) and through trains to Hereford. In 1910 there were three of these daily. The through service lasted over 50 years until 1 January 1931 when the London Midland & Scottish withdrew all its services between Brecon and Ynys-y-Geinon. Brynamman services continued, some trains running only as far as Ystalyfera. In 1938 there were eleven trains on a Saturday.

Brynamman East Station with Brynamman West Station and a train visible through the bridge, August 1958.

No. 7481 with the 12.36 p.m. to Swansea at Brynamman East Station, August 1948.

Ystalyfera Station, *c.* 1905.

Pontadawe Station, *c.* 1905.

Clydach-on-Tawe Station, *c.* **1910.**

Upper Bank Station, August 1948.

Swansea St Thomas Station, August 1948.

Swansea St Thomas Station, August 1948.

Great Western Railway: Morriston Branch

Passenger service withdrawn	11 June 1956
Distance	2 miles (Swansea Hafod Junction to Morriston)
	1.2 miles (Morriston to Felin Fran)
Company	Great Western Railway

Stations closed	*Date of closure*
Landore Low Level	4 January 1954
Plas Marl	11 June 1956
Copper Pit Halt *	11 June 1956
Morriston West **	11 June 1956
Pentrefelin	11 June 1956

*   Known as Copper Pit Platform until 1939.
**   Known as Morriston until January 1950.

The Morriston Branch, built to serve a growing area of Swansea, opened on 9 May 1881. In 1887 the service, to and from Swansea High Street, consisted of only one daily train each way in the morning and another in the afternoon although on Saturdays there were six trains each way. The fare was 5d (about two pence) first class, but only 2$\frac{1}{2}$d (about one pence) parliamentary class (these were trains required by the Railway Regulation Act of 1844, which stipulated that companies provided a minimum standard of service of at least one train per day for third class passengers).

When the Swansea avoiding line was built the branch was extended to it at Felin Fran and this extension opened on 8 May 1914. In 1922 there were four daily trains with an additional one on Saturdays.

Landore Low Level Station, June 1951.

Neath & Brecon Railway *

Passenger service withdrawn	15 October 1962
Distance	33 miles (Brecon to Neath Low Level)
Company	Neath & Brecon Railway

Stations closed	*Date of closure*
Cadoxton Terrace Halt	15 October 1962
Penscynor Halt	15 October 1962
Cilfrew Halt	15 October 1962
Cefn Coed Colliery Halt	15 October 1962
Crynant	15 October 1962
Crynant New Colliery Halt (miners)	after 1954
Brynteg Colliery Halt (miners) **	by September 1938
Seven Sisters	15 October 1962
Pantyffordd Halt	15 October 1962

*   The closed stations on his line that were in Brecknockshire were Onllwyn, Craig-y-Nos, Cray, Devynock & Sennybridge, Abercamlais Halt, Penpont Halt, Aberbran, Cradoc and Brecon Mount Street.

**   Also known as Brynteg and Nantycefn Halt.

The Neath & Brecon Railway had its origins in the Dulas Valley Mineral Railway to serve a coalfield between Neath and Onllwyn. Before that opened in October 1864 the company had changed its name to the Neath & Brecon Railway and obtained powers for a line from Onllwyn to Brecon in July 1863, which opened on 3 June 1867. A year later another Act granted powers for a line from Devynock to Llangammarch Wells where it was intended to join the Central Wales Extension Railway. This would have been a useful north–south link but it became a victim of the financial crash of 1866 and was heard of no more.

The other part of the Neath & Brecon, the line from Colbren Junction to Ynys-y-Geinon on the Swansea Vale Railway, strictly lies outside the area of this book but is included for completeness. It started life as a separate company and when the contractor building the line got into financial difficulties the Neath & Brecon took over. The Swansea Vale had obtained running powers over the Neath & Brecon so when the Midland Railway absorbed the Swansea Vale it gained access right through to Swansea. The Midland soon concluded an agreement with the Neath & Brecon to work all traffic between Brecon, Colbren Junction and Ynys-y-Geinon and also provide the staff and maintenance. In 1910 there were six daily trains between Neath and Colbren Junction and the table is listed as 'Midland and Neath and Brecon'. In view of this it might have been expected that the Neath & Brecon would have become part of the London Midland & Scottish at the Grouping, but instead it became part of the Great Western group.

No. 4653 leaving with the 4.10 p.m. Neath–Brecon from Penscynor Halt, September 1960.

Cilfrew Halt facing Neath, April 1961.

Seven Sisters Station, *c.* 1912.

M. C. B. RY. STATION, SEVENSISTERS. HARRIS, GWALIA.

Port Talbot Railway & Docks

Port Talbot (originally known as Aberavon) developed during the Industrial Revolution with the production of tinplate and copper. The Port Talbot Railway & Docks was formed in 1894 as another outlet for the ever-expanding coal industry with the advantage over Newport and Cardiff of being nearer to the open sea. Besides improving the dock facilities there was a main line, described below, and a network of lines built primarily for mineral traffic (the Tonmawr branch carried miners but I have not found a service in a public timetable) which fall outside the scope of this book. As part of moves to protect itself from the Barry Railway's intentions to expand westwards, the Great Western Railway entered into a working agreement with the Port Talbot from 1 January 1908 although the docks remained outside Great Western control. At the Grouping the Port Talbot became part of the Great Western group as a subsidiary company contributing 35 miles.

Blaengarw Line

Passenger service withdrawn	11 September 1933
Distance	13.8 miles (Port Talbot Central to Pontyrhyll Junction)
Company	Port Talbot Railway

Stations closed	*Date of closure*
Bettws (Llangeinor)	11 September 1933
Celtic Halt (workmen) *	by September 1938
Celtic Lower Platform **	after 1930
Lletty Brongu	11 September 1933
Garth	9 June 1913
Cwmdu	11 September 1933
Maesteg Neath Road ***	11 September 1933
Bryn	11 September 1933
Duffryn Mills Halt *	by September 1938
Port Talbot Central	11 September 1933

*   Workmen's halt.
**   Miners' halt; known as Cwm Cedfyw Rhondda Halt until 1924.
*** Known as Maesteg until 1 July 1924.

The Port Talbot main line was built over a summit at Maesteg to a junction with the Great Western Railway's Garw Branch at Pontyrhyll, from which point the Port Talbot Railway had running powers to Blaengarw for passenger trains but had to exchange freight at Pontyrhyll. The line opened for passengers on 14 February 1898 and involved about 3.5 miles of 1 in 40 climbing from Port Talbot (fortunately the direction for the empties) to the summit at Maesteg, but a gentler climb for westbound loaded trains of 1 in 75. The summit was in a tunnel and an automatic gong was provided to alert the crew to the change in gradient. These grades required particularly powerful locomotives and two 0-8-2Ts were provided by the American manufacturer Cooke (later part of Alco). These locomotives were known as the 'Yankee Engines' and were later joined by three similar, though slightly more powerful, locomotives built by Sharp Stewart. The passenger service was normally provided by a railmotor, which was supplied in 1907. At 77 feet long it was the largest vehicle of its type in Britain with an articulated six-coupled power unit that was sheeted over to match the coach. Another unusual feature was the electric lighting supplied by a steam turbine rather than the usual dynamo driven by a belt from one of the axles. There were also eight bogie carriages, which were used on Saturdays when the traffic was too much for the railmotor.

In 1910 there were five weekday services with an additional one on Saturdays, taking about 55 minutes for the seventeen and a half mile journey to Blaengarw. Most trains left from Port Talbot's Central Station but some left from the Port Talbot & Aberavon Station of the Rhondda & Swansea Bay Railway.

Lletty Brongu Station, July 1959.

Cwmdu Station, July 1959.

Maesteg Station, c. 1905.

P.T.R. STATION. MAESTEG.

854

Maesteg Neath Road Station, behind the trees on the upper line, July 1959. The lower line continues left to Maesteg Castle Street Station.

Bryn Station, July 1959.

Rhondda & Swansea Bay Railway

Passenger service withdrawn	11 September 1933 (Court Sart to Swansea Riverside)
	3 December 1962 (Briton Ferry to Cymmer Afan)
	26 February 1968 (Cymmer Afan to Treherbert)
Distance	24.8 miles (Swansea to Treherbert)
Company	Rhondda & Swansea Bay Railway

Stations closed	*Date of closure*
Blaen-Rhondda	26 February 1968
Blaenycwm	closure date unknown
Blaengwynfy	26 February 1968
Cymmer Afan *	15 July 1970
Duffryn Rhondda Halt **	7 November 1956
Cynonville Halt ***	2 January 1956
Pontrhydyfen	3 December 1962
Cwmavon (Glam) ****	3 December 1962
Aberavon Town *****	3 December 1962
Aberavon Seaside	3 December 1962
Baglan Sands Halt †	25 September 1939
Briton Ferry East ††	16 September 1935
Court Sart	16 September 1935
Cape Platform †††	11 September 1933
Jersey Marine	11 September 1933
Baldwin's Halt	11 September 1933
Danygraig	11 September 1933
Swansea Riverside ††††	11 September 1933
Port Talbot Docks	14 March 1895

*	Known as Cymmer until 1906, as Cymmer for Glyncorrwg until 1 July 1924 and as Cwm Cymmer until 17 September 1926. Amalgamated with Cymmer General in January 1950.
**	This halt opened in October 1912 on the site of the old Duffryn Rhondda Platform which had closed in October 1911.
***	This halt opened in October 1912 on the site of the old Cynon Colliery which had closed in October 1911.
****	Known as Cwmavon until 1 January 1902
*****	Known as Aberavon until 1 December 1891, as Aberavon & Port Talbot until June 1895, and as Port Talbot (Aberavon) until 1 July 1924.
†	Closed between 26 September 1938 and 29 May 1939.
††	Known as Briton Ferry until 1 July 1924.
†††	Known as Cape Halt until 1920.
††††	Known as Swansea until 1 July 1924 and Swansea Docks until 17 September 1926.

When the Prince of Wales Dock opened in Swansea in October 1881, it was hoped that some of the mineral wealth of the Rhondda could be diverted to Swansea. The town had the advantage of being 40 miles closer to the open sea than Cardiff but against this had to be set the obstacle of a high ridge which had to be crossed. The first proposal was to use the South Wales Mineral Railway to Glyncorrwg and then drive a tunnel into the Rhondda Valley and build a bridge over the river at Neath and so into Swansea. Another proposal involved building a line from a junction with the Taff Vale Railway at Treherbert, use of a tunnel into the Afon Valley and down to Pontrhydyfen, and then bridging the mouth of the Neath River into Swansea. Interests in Neath opposed the bridge across the river and led to the line being sanctioned only to Briton Ferry, a line from Pontrhydyfen to Port Talbot also being approved. Approval for a line into Swansea was not obtained until 1891. The line opened between Aberavon and Cymmer in November 1885 and to Port Talbot in 1891. When the Swansea extension opened on 14 March 1895 the Port Talbot station closed to passengers. The tunnel through into the Rhondda Valley did not open until 2 July 1890. It was the longest tunnel in Wales at 3,443 yards (almost two miles) and took almost three years to build.

The Great Western took over working the line from July 1906 and it became a subsidiary of that company in 1922. In September 1933 trains were diverted into Swansea East Dock Station (and later to High Street) with consequent closure of stations west of Court Sart. Passenger trains ceased when the Rhondda tunnel was closed in February 1968 due to earth movements but buses provided a service until the official closure date of 14 December 1970 (by which time the service was via Cymmer Afan from Bridgend).

Blean-Rhondda Station, *c.* 1910.

Blaengwynfy Station, November 1957.

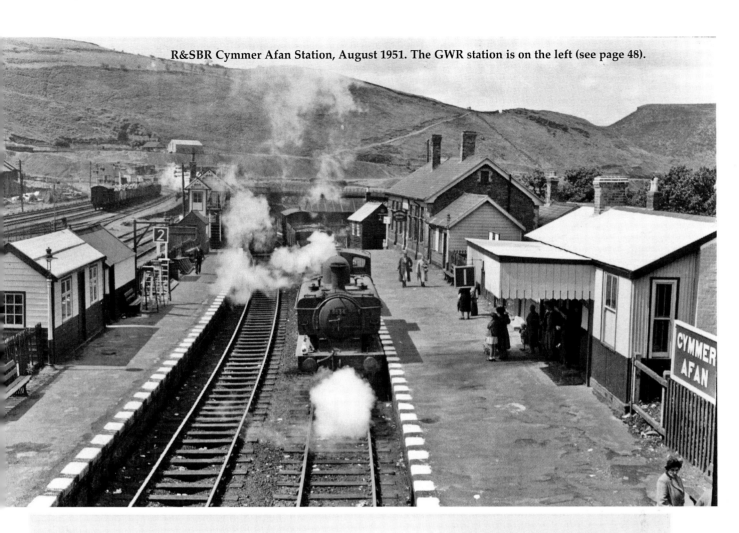

R&SBR Cymmer Afan Station, August 1951. The GWR station is on the left (see page 48).

Pontrhydyfen Station, September 1960.

Cwmavon Station, *c.* 1910.

Aberavon Station, *c.* 1905.

Neath Branch

Passenger service withdrawn	16 September 1935
Distance	1.6 miles (Court Sart to Neath)
Company	Rhondda & Swansea Bay Railway

Stations closed	*Date of closure*
Neath Canal Side *	16 September 1935

* Known as Neath until 1 July 1924 and Neath Canal Bridge until 17 September 1926.

This branch opened on 14 December 1894 from a junction with the main line at Court Sart. In 1910 there was a departure from Neath to connect with each daily main-line train and a corresponding return working. It was obviously felt that the people of Neath were God-fearing folk as no connection was provided for the two Sunday trains!

Neath Canal Side Station, *c.* **1912.**

Rhymney Railway

The Rhymney Railway gained its Act in July 1854 and was intended to link the coalfields of the Rhymney Valley with Cardiff. The original line used running powers over the Taff Vale Railway but this was unsatisfactory and in 1864 the Rhymney obtained powers for its own independent line into Cardiff which opened in 1871. At the same time a new station was built in Caerphilly and passenger traffic no longer used the Caerphilly–Walnut Tree Junction line where it connected with the Taff Vale. Interestingly it adopted flat bottom rails when built, only later adopting what was the then standard bullhead or double head type of rail.

The Rhymney Railway became part of the Great Western group in 1923, contributing 51 route miles. The shareholders had done very well, having received a dividend of 9% for many years. They should probably have thanked Mr Cornelius Lundie, a Scot born at Kelso in 1815. He joined the Rhymney in 1863 and continued as general manager until 1904 when, at 89, he accepted lighter duties! He died in 1908. When the new group decided to concentrate locomotive maintenance facilities for South Wales in one place the Rhymney's works at Caerphilly were chosen. The Rhymney Main Line (Rhymney to Cardiff) still provides services to Rhymney and so is listed in the section 'Closed passenger stations on lines still open' later in this book. However, the Rhymney had a number of branches which have not survived and which warrant further description. Joint lines with the Great Western and London & North Western railways are also presented here.

Rhymney Main Line (Running Powers)

Stations closed	Date of closure
Caerphilly *	1 April 1871
Cardiff Adam Street **	1st April 1871

* Replaced by new station on opening of own line to Cardiff.
** Replaced by Crockherbtown on opening of own line from Caerphilly.

These stations were used when running powers were required over the Taff Vale Railway, but were closed when the Rhymney's own main line to Cardiff opened in 1871.

Senghenydd Branch

Passenger service withdrawn	15 June 1964
Distance	3.4 miles (Aber Branch Junction to Senghenydd)
Company	Rhymney Railway

Stations closed	Date of closure
Penyrheol	15 June 1964
Abertridwr *	15 June 1964
Windsor Colliery Halt **	15 June 1964
Senghenydd ***	15 June 1964

* Known as Aber until 26 June 1899.
** Workmen's halt.
*** Known as Senghenith until 1 July 1904.

This line opened on 1 February 1894 although a length of about half a mile had been open previously as far as Tirgibbon Colliery. In 1910 the service (worked at that time by one of two railmotors) consisted of up to nine trains during the week with more on Saturdays although, of course, none on Sunday. It took fifteen minutes for the four mile journey from Caerphilly. By 1938 most trains on the branch were working to and from Cardiff, taking about 45 minutes for the journey.

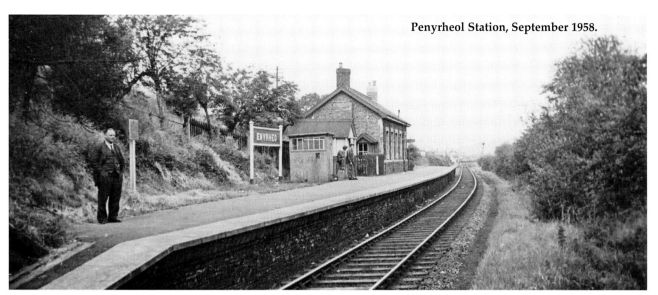

Penyrheol Station, September 1958.

Abertridwr Station, *c.* 1900.

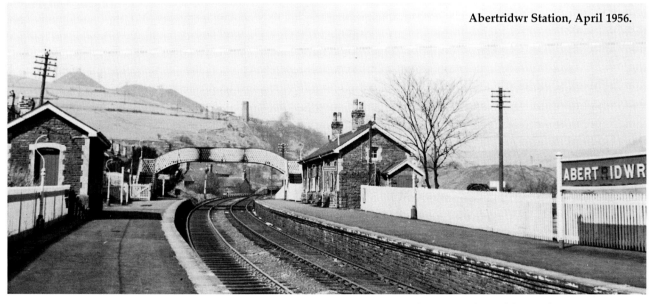

Abertridwr Station, April 1956.

Senghenydd Station, *c.* 1910.

Senghenydd Station, *c.* 1910.

Deri Junction Branch

Passenger service withdrawn	31 December 1962
Distance	2.4 miles (Bargoed to Deri Junction)
Company	Rhymney Railway

Stations closed	*Date of closure*
Darran & Deri *	31 December 1962
Groesfaen Colliery Platform **	31 December 1962

* Known as Darran until 1 August 1868.
** Known as Groesfaen Colliers' Platform until September 1938.

Powers to construct this branch were obtained in 1861 and it opened in 1865 to Deri Junction where it made an end-on connection to the Brecon & Merthyr Railway and formed a link in that company's route to Newport. As that company provided most of the mileage and ran the passenger service on the line it is considered in that section.

Darran & Deri Station, October 1952.

Rhymney Bridge Extension

Passenger service withdrawn	21 September 1953
Distance	1.5 miles (Rhymney to Rhymney Bridge)
Company	Rhymney Railway and London & North Western Railway

Stations closed	*Date of closure*
Cemetery Road Halt	by September1928

The same Act that granted powers for the Rhymney's Cardiff line granted powers for a northern extension from Rhymney to the gradually extending London & North Western Heads of Valleys line at Nantybwch. In 1867 agreement was reached with the London & North Western by which the extension became a joint line. It opened on 5 September 1871 and had a major effect on goods traffic to the Midlands and the North which had previously gone via the Great Western's Taff Vale extension line at Hengoed. With the new line goods traffic was passed north to the London & North Western, increasing the proportion of Rhymney Railway receipts. The London & North Western gained running powers to Cardiff and opened its own goods depot in Bute East Docks in 1875. At one time the London & North Western was running six goods trains daily between Cardiff and Abergavenny. In addition the company provided through coaches between Cardiff and Liverpool and Manchester which lasted until the start of the First World War.

Penallta Branch

Distance	1.2 miles (Ystrad Mynach to Penallta Junction)
Company	Rhymney Railway

This short line connecting the Rhymney to the Great Western's Taff Vale Extension line at Penallta Junction opened in September 1871. Running powers were granted over the Great Western to the collieries in the Aberdare Valley. Crucially, this line gave access to two joint lines which were to be built with the Great Western. There were no passenger stations on this line.

Rhymney Railway and Great Western Railway
Taff Bargoed Railway

Passenger service withdrawn	15 June 1964
Distance	9.2 miles (Dowlais Cae Harris to Llancaiach)
Company	Rhymney Railway and Great Western Railway

Stations closed	*Date of closure*
Dowlais Cae Harris	15 June 1964
Penydarren Platform †	after 1954
Cwm Bargoed †	15 June 1964
Nantyffyn †	after June 1954
Bedlinog Colliery Junction †*	after June 1954
Bedlinog	15 June 1964
Nantwen Colliery **	after 1928
Taff Merthyr Colliery Halt	15 June 1964
Trelewis Platform	15 June 1964

† Miners' halts.
* Closed between November 1915 and 1938.
** Known as Nantwen until November 1915

Following an agreement with the Great Western Railway in 1867, the Taff Bargoed was built from the Great Western line at Llancaiach and opened to passengers on 1 February 1876. Its main purpose was not passenger traffic but the rich rewards to be gained from the iron ore traffic to the Dowlais Iron Company and the line opened for mineral traffic on 10 January 1876. The almost one and a half mile Dowlais Zigzag lines (there were two sections) brought rail traffic right into the iron works. The line had a significant effect on the Rhymney's finances: no dividend had been paid in 1875 but rose to 11% in 1881 and 1882.

The route to Dowlais was hard but in 1913 the Rhymney hauled 400,000 tons of ore to the furnaces up a gradient of between 1 in 40 and 1 in 49 for seven miles using three locomotives for a 20-wagon train and taking 40 minutes. Passenger services were run jointly with the Great Western from Llancaiach and in 1887 there were three trains daily each way, becoming five by 1910. By 1938 there were seven trains daily but no Sunday service.

No. 5674 with an NCB miner's train at Dowlais Cae Harris, August 1951.

Cwm Bargoed Station, July 1958.

Bedlinog Station, September 1960.

Rhymney Railway and Great Western Railway: Taff Bargoed Railway

Quaker's Yard & Merthyr Line

Passenger service withdrawn	12 February 1951
Distance	5.9 miles (Quaker's Yard to Cyfarthfa Junction)
Company	Rhymney Railway and Great Western Railway

Stations closed	Date of closure
Abercanaid *	12 February1951
Gethin Pit Platform †	by September 1928
Castle Pit †	after 1915
Troedyrhiw Platform	12 February1951
Aberfan **	12 February1951
Pontygwaith Halt	12 February1951

†   Miners' halts.
*   Known as Abercanaid & Pentrebach between 9 September 1913 and 1 July 1924.
**   Known as Aberfan for Merthyr Vale between January 1902 and July 1932.

This was the second of the two Great Western joint lines opened to passengers on 1 April 1886 from a junction with the Great Western's Taff Vale Extension line at Quaker's Yard High Level. The line closely followed the route of the existing Taff Vale Railway line to Merthyr with the aim of tapping some of that company's traffic. In 1887 there were five daily trains each way working to and from Cardiff and two on Sundays. By 1910 there was a basic daily service of nine trains, some of which were operated by one of the Rhymney's two railmotors. By 1938 there were eight trains daily, some of them commencing at Nelson & Llancaiach or Quaker's Yard rather than Cardiff.

Abercanaid Station, *c.* **1904.**

Aberfan Station, *c.* **1908.**

South Wales Mineral Railway

Passenger service withdrawn	22 September 1930
Distance	2.8 miles (Cymmer to Glyncorrwg)
Company	South Wales Mineral Railway

Stations closed	*Date of closure*
North Rhondda Halt	22 September 1930
South Pit Halt *	22 September 1930
Glyncorrwg	22 September 1930
Nantewlaeth Halt **	closed after 1954
Cymmer Corrwg ***	22 September 1930

*   Earlier known as Glyncorrwg South Pits Halt.
**   Miners' halt.
*** Known as Cymmer until 17 September 1926.

The South Wales Mineral Railway was authorised in August 1853 to build a thirteen-mile broad gauge line from Briton Ferry to Glyncorrwg. A one-and-a-half-mile cable-worked incline brought the railway down to the South Wales Railway at Briton Ferry. The railway opened in 1863 and was converted to standard gauge in 1873. It was initially worked by the Glyncorrwg Coal Company and when that company failed it passed into the hands of the Official Receiver for many years. In 1898 the Port Talbot's branches to Blaenavon and Whitworth opened and much traffic was diverted over these lines away from the South Wales Mineral Line. Working passed to the Port Talbot company in 1908 and a passenger service from Cymmer to North Rhondda ran from March 1918. In 1922 Bradshaw shows only two trains a day timed to do the journey in eight minutes up or six minutes down but North Rhondda is not shown in the timetable. After the line closed workmen's trains continued into the 1960s when it was said to be the steepest line (at 1 in 22) on British Railways with a passenger service.

There is also a reference to a Cymmer to Glyncorrwg passenger service inaugurated in 1880 but details of it are scanty: Bradshaw does not mention it in 1887 and the 1910 timetable lists Cymmer as the station for Glyncorrwg, two and a half miles away, although neglects to mention how to get there!

No. 9617 with a workman's train at North Rhondda Halt, July 1958.

Glyncorrwg Station, July 1959.

Nantewlaeth Colliery Halt, July 1959.

Cymmer Corrwg, August 1951.

Swansea & Mumbles Railway

Passenger service withdrawn	6 January 1960
Distance	5.5 miles
Company	Oystermouth Railway

Stations closed	*Date of closure*
Swansea Rutland Street *	6 January 1960
Argyle Street *	about 1887
St Helens Road *	6 January 1960
Waterworks Road	after May 1869.
St Gabriels *	sometime in 1912
Bryn Mill *	6 January 1960
Sketty Road *	closed by 1929
Ashleigh Road	6 January 1960
Mumbles Road *	6 January 1960
Blackpill *†	6 January 1960
Bishopston Road	after May 1869
Lilliput *	sometime in 1900
West Cross *	6 January 1960
Norton Road * ††	6 January 1960
Oystermouth *	6 January 1960
Southend	6 January 1960
Mumbles Pier †††	11 October 1959

*   Closed between 1827 and 1860.
†   Known originally as Black Pill, date of change unknown.
††   Later closed but reopened in 1929.
††† Originally known as Mumbles.

The Oystermouth Railway can be counted as the fifth oldest railway built with Parliamentary powers, which were granted by Act of 29 June 1804. Interestingly, the company was granted powers to use mechanical means of propulsion at this early date although it opened as a horse-worked plateway. It seems to have opened, at least in part, for goods traffic (coal and lime were important items) in April 1806. Although not specifically allowed for in the Act, the line started carrying passengers on 25 March 1807 – a world first – at a fare of 1s (five pence). In 1826 a turnpike was built between Oystermouth and Swansea and competition from horse buses caused the rail passenger service to be withdrawn – an ominous precedent. However, by 1860 the line had been rebuilt with edge rails and the passenger service reinstated.

Steam traction was introduced in 1877 and, because the line had much of the character of a roadside tramway, the earliest locomotives were of the steam tram type. This was the earliest use of tramway locomotives on a street line. In 1874 the Swansea Improvements & Tramways Company was formed and its Act gave it running powers over the line to Oystermouth. Although one company running over another's line was common, this case was unusual as the tramway company operated a horsedrawn service although the railway's services were steam hauled. Not that the tramway did not want to operate steam services but the railway company prevented it from doing so. This situation finally came to an end in March 1896 when the tramway company was compensated for forgoing its running powers.

In August 1889 an Act was obtained to extend the line to Mumbles and build a pier. The line and pier opened on 10 May 1898. Authority was also obtained to extend the new line from Oystermouth to Blackpill which resulted in the roadside alignment being abandoned for a new one on the seashore. In 1925 an order was made allowing the line to use electric traction and a public electric service began on 2 March 1929 using Brush-built tramway style cars. These large cars could seat 106 passengers. Later that year a petrol locomotive was introduced for goods traffic. The line appeared to have been very scenic with roadside and seashore running and might well have been preserved if it had survived a few more years.

No. 8 with a train at St Helens Road Station.

50247 MUMBLES TRAIN AT ST HELEN'S JUNCTION

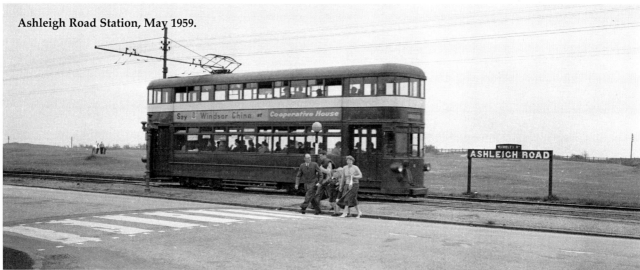

Ashleigh Road Station, May 1959.

A train near Mumbles Road Station, May 1959.

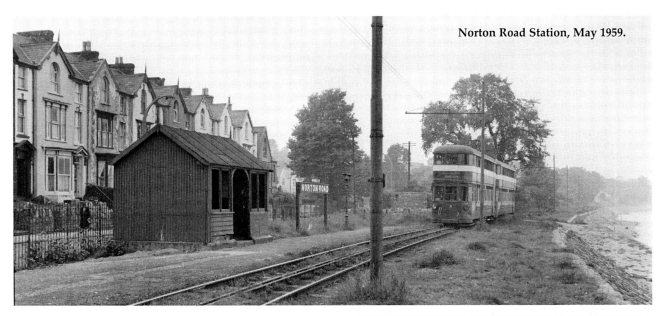

Norton Road Station, May 1959.

Oystermouth Station, 1907.

Oystermouth Station, May 1959.

Southend Station, *c.* 1920.

Mumbles Pier Station, *c.* 1905.

Swansea District Lines (Great Western Railway) I

Passenger service withdrawn	22 September 1924
Distance	10.8 miles (Skewen East Junction to Morlais Junction South)
Company	Great Western Railway

Stations closed	*Date of closure*
Pont Lliw	22 September 1924
Llangyfelach	22 September 1924
Felin Fran Halt	11 June 19569

At the beginning of the twentieth century the Great Western Railway modernised itself. Not only were there new locomotives and rolling stock, but new major routes came into operation, such as the Paddington to Birmingham direct line and the Bristol to Birmingham line, dispelling the old slur that GWR stood for 'great way round' (the cognoscenti always knew it stood for 'God's Wonderful Railway'!) The railway to South Wales benefited by a new direct line to the Severn Tunnel and the work to develop the harbour at Fishguard for both Irish and Atlantic traffic. The last of the cut-off lines to be built before the First World War were the Swansea District Lines, conceived to avoid the two-mile climb, mostly at 1 in 52, from Landore to Crockett tunnel on the South Wales main line, which often needed a banking locomotive. Up trains also had a sharp climb from Gowerton. Powers to build these lines were granted by an Act of August 1904.

At the western end of the new line a short line was constructed to join the Llanelly Railway in the northerly direction to facilitate the passage of mineral trains and the Morriston branch was extended to Felin Fran on the new line. The avoiding line opened throughout on 14 July 1913. The stations at Pont Lliw and Llangyfelach were short-lived, having opened only on 9 July 1923.

Swansea District Lines (Great Western Railway) II

Passenger service withdrawn	4 October 1947
Distance	2.3 miles (Lonlas Junction to Jersey Marine South Junction)
Company	Great Western Railway

Stations closed	*Date of closure*
Llandarcy Platform	4 October 1947

This line was built from the avoiding line, near Skewen, to the Swansea & Neath line to provide easy access to Swansea Docks; it opened on 18 February 1912. To avoid the detour into Neath a loop was opened on 9 May 1915 from this line to join the Rhondda & Swansea Bay Railway, over which the Great Western had running powers. Trains stopping at Llandarcy Platform were through trains from the Morriston branch to Briton Ferry or Port Talbot. This line and the avoiding line continued to carry through passenger traffic after their stations had closed but they are now open only for goods.

The short lived Roath Statio in Cardiff lasted from 1899 to 1917, seen here *c.* 1905.

Taff Vale Railway

Industry developed comparatively early around Merthyr Tydfil with several ironworks established before the beginning of the nineteenth century. These industries needed transport both to move the product to market and to bring in raw materials – by the 1830s demand for iron ore was such that it, too, needed to be brought in to supplement local supplies. The Glamorganshire Canal gained its Act in June 1790; it opened in 1789 and rose almost 570 feet in the 25 miles from Cardiff to Merthyr. As traffic increased proposals were made to build a railway between Cardiff and Merthyr and a friend of Brunel's asked him to prepare an estimate of the cost of such a line. As a consequence the Taff Vale Railway obtained its Act on 21 June 1836 despite opposition from the canal company. Brunel was the engineer and, most unusually, built the line to four feet, eight and a half inch gauge rather than broad gauge. This was probably to take account of the difficult terrain the line was to pass through.

As built the overall gradient of the line was fairly gentle except for a section between Navigation House and Quakers' Yard. Here Brunel used stationary winding engines to assist trains up half a mile as steep as 1 in 19. This continued until 1864 when a diversion with a gradient of 1 in 40 was brought into use and locomotives could be used throughout. The line opened as far as Abercynon on 9 October 1840 and on to Merthyr on 12 April 1841. The line is the only one of six still open to Merthyr and so appears in the section on lines still open.

The Taff Vale developed much further and acquired a number of other companies so that by the time it became a constituent of the Great Western group it contributed a total of 124 1/2 route miles. It was also successful financially, at one time paying a dividend of 17 1/2%.

Porth to Maerdy

Passenger service withdrawn	15 June 1964
Distance	6.4 miles (Porth to Maerdy)
Company	Taff Vale Railway
Stations closed	*Date of closure*
Maerdy	15 June 1964
Ferndale	15 June 1964
Tylorstown *	15 June 1964
Wattstown Platform	12 July 1920
Ynyshir **	15 June 1964

*   Renamed from Tylor's Town by 1904.
**   Earlier known as Ynishir.

The Taff Vale had obtained powers to extend into the Rhondda in 1846 but was cautious about doing so in the wake of the financial crisis of 1845. The company tried to stimulate discoveries of coal in the upper part of the Rhondda by offering an award of £500 for the discovery of coal in the Treherbert area. The line to Maerdy came about in stages. First a short section in 1849 from Porth to Ynyshir and then on to Ferndale in 1856. Maerdy (the highest point on the Taff Vale at 900 feet) was reached by the purchase of a private railway but at first the line was open only for mineral traffic. Passenger traffic to Ferndale began in 1876 and to Maerdy only in 1889. By 1910 there was an intensive service with no less than seventeen trains to Maerdy on weekdays (with an additional one on Saturdays) and, unusually, a Sunday service of five trains. There had been some reduction in services by 1922 which suggests road competition was already being felt.

The train for Porth at Maerdy Station, March 1951.

Maerdy Station, *c*. 1910.

Ferndale Station, *c*. 1905.

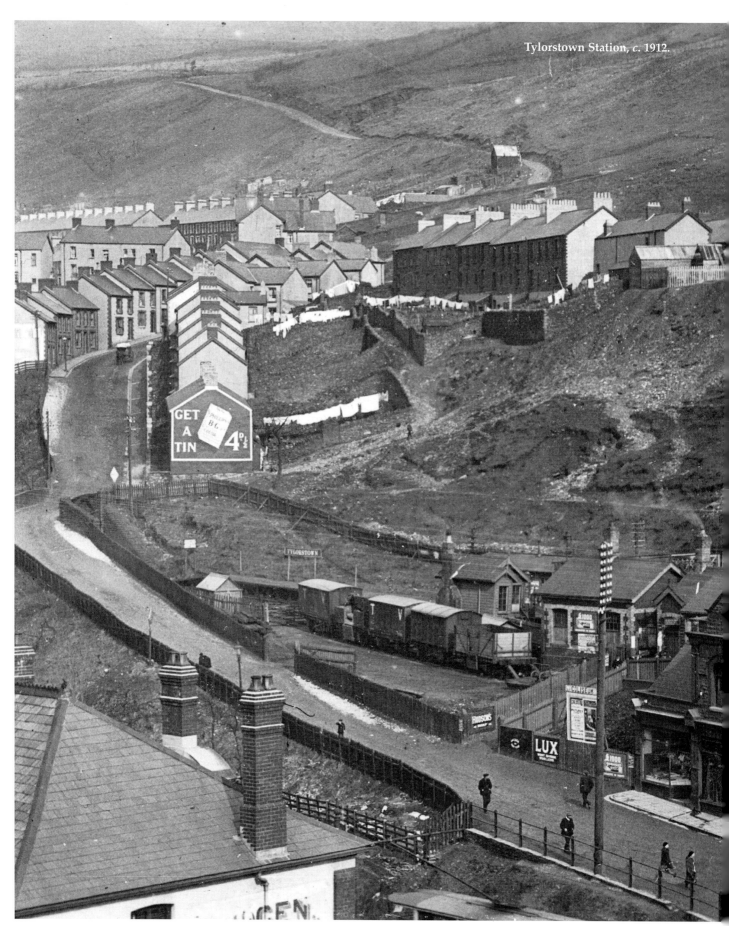

Tylorstown Station, *c.* 1912.

Ynysybwl Branch

Passenger service withdrawn	28 July 1952
Distance	3.4 miles (Ynysybwl branch Junction to Old Ynysybwl Halt)
Company	Taff Vale Railway

Stations closed	*Date of closure*
Old Ynysybwl Halt *	28 July 1952
Ynysbwl	28 July 1952
Robertstown Halt **	28 July 1952
Ynysybwl New Road Halt ***	28 July 1952
Clydach Court Halt ****	28 July 1952

*   Known as Old Ynysybwl Platform until 2 October 1922.
**   Known as Robertstown Platform until 2 October 1922.
***   Known as Ynysybwl New Road until 7 May 1945 and before that as Ynysybwl New Road Platform.
**** Known as Clydach Court Platform until 2 October 1922.

This line opened to Ynysybwl for goods in 1886 and for passengers in March 1890. Services were extended to Old Ynysybwl in November 1905. As built, the branch junction faced towards Merthyr but in 1900 the Ynysbwl Junction South Curve was opened and this allowed a direct run for trains from Pontypridd to Ynysybwl, passenger services beginning on this line on 1 November 1904. In 1910 there was an intensive service of twelve daily railmotor trains, with five additional ones on Saturdays, taking about fifteen minutes for the journey from Pontypridd. The track beyond Old Ynysybwl Halt to Llanwonno Colliery was lifted in December 1938.

No. 6411 and auto-trailer 114 with the 4.23 p.m. from Pontypridd at Old Ynysybwl Halt, September 1951.

Nelson Branch

Passenger service withdrawn	12 September 1932
Distance	5 miles (Pontypridd to Nelson)
Company	Taff Vale Railway

Stations closed	*Date of closure*
Nelson (Glam) *	12 September 1932
Llanfabon Road Halt **	12 September 1932
Traveller's Rest ***	12 September 1932
Cilfynydd	12 September 1932
Coedpenmaen ****	12 September 1932
Berw Road Halt *****	12 September 1932

*	Known as Nelson until 1 July 1924.
**	Known as Llanfabon Road Platform until 2 October 1922.
***	Known as Traveller's Rest (Abercynon Upper) until 1 July 1924.
****	The official closure date is given but the last train called here on 1 June 1915.
*****	Known as Berw Road Platform until 2 October 1922, this station replaced an earlier station of the same name in July 1908.

The Llancaiach branch opened from a junction with the main line at Stormstown Junction in 1841 but in this form did not carry passengers. However, in 1887 a new branch was built from a junction with the main line almost a mile north of Pontypridd along the east side of the Taff to a colliery near Cilfynydd and in 1900 the line was extended to form a loop by joining the original Llancaiach branch at Ynysydwr Junction. Passenger services to Nelson began along this line on 1 June 1900. Although the line made a junction with the Great Western's Taff Vale Extension line this was only used for goods traffic and passenger trains did not run to the Great Western station (Nelson & Llancaiach) despite the company having decided in 1930 to upgrade the quarter mile between the stations for passenger working. In 1910 there were nine railmotor trains daily with an additional one on Saturdays.

The Taff Vale was an enthusiastic user of railmotors with a total of sixteen. They were unusual in having twin transverse boilers which were good steam producers, particularly from cold. The locomotive part was numbered separately from the coach part and as there were two spare engine units railmotors numbered up to eighteen could be seen.

A railmotor at Nelson Station.

Llantrisant Branch

Passenger service withdrawn	31 March 1952
Distance	5.3 miles (Llantrisant Junction to Maesaraul Junction)
Company	Llantrisant & Taff Vale Junction Railway

Stations closed	*Date of closure*
Tonteg Halt *	31 March 1952
Church Village Halt **	31 March 1952
Llantwit Fardre ***	31 March 1952
Beddau Halt ****	31 March 1952
Cross Inn	31 March 1952

*   This halt replaced an earlier one of the same name which had been known as Tonteg Platform until 1 October 1923.
**   Known as Church Village until 14 March 1932.
***   Known as Llantwit until 8 October 1936.
**** Known as Beddau Platform until 1 October 1923.

The Llantrisant & Taff Vale Junction Railway was promoted by the Taff Vale and obtained powers in June 1861 for a line, using the Llantwit Vardre Tramroad, from the Taff Vale at Llantisant Branch Junction near Treforest to a junction with the broad gauge Ely Valley Railway Brofiskin branch at Maesaraul over which it had running powers into Llantrisant, the exercise of which required that a third rail be laid. The line was leased by the Taff Vale from its opening in 1863 for goods and 1865 for passengers. In 1889 the line was amalgamated with the Taff Vale.

Church Village Halt, July 1959.

Cross Inn Station, July 1959.

Cowbridge Railway

Passenger service withdrawn	26 November 1951
Distance	5.6 miles (Llantrisant to Cowbridge)
Company	Cowbridge Railway

Stations closed	*Date of closure*
Llantrisant *	2 November 1964
Llanharry	26 November 1951
Ystradowen	26 November 1951
Trerhyngyll & Maendy Platform	26 November 1951
Aberthin Platform	12 July 1920
Cowbridge **	26 November 1951

*   Renamed from Llantrissant by 1902; the original Cowbridge station was amalgamated with the Great Western one on 21 September 1925.

**   Replaced the first Cowbridge station when the line was extended on 1 October 1892.

The Cowbridge Railway was a local company promoted with Taff Vale support to connect the town of Cowbridge to the railway network. The line gained its Act in July 1862 and opened for passengers in September 1865. At first the company worked its own trains, with hired locomotives, despite a working agreement with the Great Western having been reached in 1873. The Taff Vale leased the line in 1876 and took over working, trains from Pontypridd having to reverse and shunt over the Great Western line at Llantrisant. It was amalgamated with the Taff Vale in August 1889. In 1887 there were four trains daily taking just under an hour for the fifteen and a half miles from Pontypridd.

Llanharry Station, July 1959.

Ystradowen Station, *c.* 1900.

Trerhyngyll & Maendy Platform with its classic Great Western corrugated iron pagoda shelter, July 1959.

The remains of Aberthin Platform , July 1959.

The platform and low shed of the old Cowbridge Station, July 1959.

An auto-train at Cowbridge Station, August 1951.

Cowbridge & Aberthaw Railway

Passenger service withdrawn	5 May 1930
Distance	6.4 miles (Cowbridge to Aberthaw)
Company	Cowbridge & Aberthaw Railway

Stations closed	*Date of closure*
St Hilary Platform	12 July 1920
St Mary Church Road *	5 May 1930
Llanbethery Platform	12 July 1920
St Athan Road *	5 May 1930
Aberthaw Low Level *	5 May 1930

* Closed between 4 May 1926 and 11 July 1927.

The Cowbridge & Aberthaw Railway was inaugurated on 1 August 1889. The line was conceived with Taff Vale backing to counter a perceived threat from the Barry Railway's Vale of Glamorgan line; it opened on 1 October 1892 and the company became part of the Taff Vale in 1895. The line was closed temporarily between 4 May 1926 and 11 July 1927. Train services worked through from Pontypridd and there were four down trains and five up in 1910.

Cadoxton Branch

Passenger service withdrawn	6 May 1968
Distance	4.7 miles (Penarth Town to Biglis Junction)
Company	Cardiff, Penarth & Barry Junction Railway

Stations closed	*Date of closure*
Sully	6 May 1968
Swanbridge Halt	6 May 1968
Lavernock	6 May 1968
Lower Penarth Halt *	14 June 1954
Alberta Place Halt **	6 May 1968

*   Known as Lower Penarth until 30 September 1935.
**   Known as Alberta Place Platform until 1 October 1923.

The Penarth Extension Railway, promoted by the Taff Vale, opened to Penarth Town in 1878. When the Barry Railway promoted its scheme to establish a new port on Barry Sound established interests felt themselves threatened and the Taff Vale responded with two schemes under the auspices of the Cardiff, Penarth & Barry Junction Railway. The scheme for a direct line to Barry failed to win approval while the coast line scheme was approved with the proviso it was only to be used for coastal traffic. The line opened in December 1888. Trains ran through to the Barry Railway station at Cadoxton and the section from Cardiff to Penarth is still open.

Sully Station, *c.* 1905

Sully Station, *c.* 1912.

Lavernock Station.

A two car auto-train leaving Alberta Place Halt.

Stations closed on lines still open to passengers
South Wales Main Line

Stations closed	Date
Ely (Main Line) *	10 September 1962
St Fagan's	10 September 1962
Peterston	2 November 1964
Llantrisant **	2 November 1964
Llanharan	2 November 1964
Tremains Factory Halt ***	c. 1963
Margam ****	2 November 1964
Briton Ferry *****	2 November 1964
Neath †	1877
Skewen ††	1 May 1910
Landore †††	2 November 1964
Cockett	15 June 1964
Loughor	4 April 1960

*   Known as Ely for Llandaff until 1 July 1924.
**   Known as Llantrissant for Cowbridge until about 1866 and a Llantrissant until about 1902.
***   Known as Tremains Platform until 2 January 1958.
****   Workmen's halt.
***** This station replaced Briton Ferry West about 600 yards south on 8 July 1935.
†   This station replaced an earlier one on the opposite side of the river in 1865 and was, in its turn, replaced by a station close to the first one in 1877 which later became Neath General.
††   Known as Dynevor until 1 October 1904 and replaced by a second station about 550 yards to the east in May 1910.
†††   Known as Landore Ticket Platform until February 1854.

Llantrisant Station, _c._ 1905.

Briton Ferry, _c._ 1910.

Rhymney Main Line
(Cardiff to Rhymney)

Stations closed	Date
Cardiff Parade *	15 April 1928
Cefn-Onn **	29 September 1926
Pwll-y-Pant	1 March 1893
Llanbradach Colliery Halt	by June 1954
Troedyrhiwfuwch Halt	1 January 1916
Pontlottyn Colliery Platform	by September 1928

*   This station replaced Adam Street station on 1 April 1871 and was known as Crockherbtown until November 1888 and as Cardiff (Rhymney Station) until 1 July 1924.

** Originally known as Cefn Coed Colliery Halt and later as Cefn On Halt until 5 May 1969 and Cefn On until 12 May 1980.

Taff Vale Main Line
(Cardiff to Merthyr)

Stations closed	Date
Woodville Road Halt *	15 September 1958
Maindy Halt **	15 September 1958
Pentyrch	June 1863
Pontygwaith Platform	1 October 1914
Dowlais Junction	May 1954

*   Known as Cathays (Woodville Road) Halt until 15 September 1952.

** Known as Maindy North Road Platform until 10 July 1922 and as Maindy North Road Halt until 15 September 1952.

The departure platform of Cardiff Parade Station.

Cefn On Halt, July 1956.

Aberdare Branch
(Taff Vale Railway)

Stations closed	Date
Pontcynon Halt *	16 March 1964
Matthewstown Halt **	16 March 1963
Penrikyber Colliery	date of closure unknown
Abercwmboi Halt	2 October 1922
Aberaman ***	16 March 1964
Commercial Street Platform	June 1912

*   Known as Pontcynon Bridge Platform until January 1910, as Pontcynon Bridge Platform until 2 October 1922 and as Pontcynon Bridge Halt until 8 June 1953.

**   Known as Matthewstown Platform until 2 October 1922.

***   Known as Treaman until August 1889. There was an earlier Aberaman Station which closed in June 1856.

Treherbert Branch
(Taff Vale Railway)

Stations closed	Date
Incline Top *	December 1857
Pandy	2 August 1886
Gelli Halt **	date of closure unknown
Pentre Platform	November 1912
Tylacoch Platform	November 1912

*   Also known as Top of Incline.

**   Known as Gelli Platform until November 1912 when it was also closed to general public use.

Aberaman Station, *c.* 1905.

Reconstruction of the platform at Aberaman Station possibly due to subsidence damage caused by mining.

Barry Pier Station looking north.

Cardiff to Bridgend/ Barry Island/Penarth

Stations closed	*Date*
Barry Pier	19 October 1971
Llandough Platform	1 June 1918

Paddle steamers *Gwalia* and *Barry* at Barry Pier, *c.* 1905.

BARRY PIER